P O C K E T S

BIRDS

TAWNY
OWL
FEATHER

EAGLE
OWL
FEATHER

EUROPEAN
EAGLE OWL

P O C K E T S

BIRDS

WRITTEN BY
BARBARA TAYLOR

ECLECTUS
PARROTS

WOODPECKER
SKULL

GREAT
WHITE
PELICAN

DK

LONDON, NEW YORK,
MUNICH, MELBOURNE, and DELHI

Project editor Miranda Smith
Art editor Helen Senior
Senior editor Susan McKeever
Designer Alexandra Brown
Editorial consultant Peter Colston
Picture research Caroline Brooke
Production Louise Barratt

REVISED EDITION
Project editor Sadie Smith
Designer Darren Holt
Managing editor Linda Esposito
Managing art editor Jane Thomas
DTP designer Siu Yin Ho
Consultant Douglas G. D. Russell B.Sc. FLS
Production Erica Rosen

First American Edition, 1995
Second American Edition, 2004
Published in the United States by
DK Publishing, Inc., 375 Hudson Street,
New York, New York 10014

05 06 07 08 09 10 9 8 7 6 5 4

ISBN 0-7566-0203-3

Color reproduction by Colourscan, Singapore
Printed and bound in Italy by L.E.G.O.
Discover more at
www.dk.com

CONTENTS

HOW TO USE THIS BOOK

These pages show you how to use *Pockets: Birds*.
The book is divided into several sections. The main
section consists of information on birds from different
habitats. There is also an introductory section at the
front, and a reference section at the back. Each new
section begins with a picture page.

HABITATS
The birds in the book are arranged
into habitats. In each habitat
section, you will find information
on the habitat, and examples of
the types of birds that live there.

Corner coding

Heading

Introduction

Caption

RIVERS, LAKES, AND SWAMPS

DUCKS
WEBBED FEET and broad, flat bills are distinctive
features of ducks. These birds are good swimmers and
strong fliers. There are two main types of duck –
dabbling ducks, such as the mallard,
that feed on the surface, and diving
ducks, such as the pochard. Many
ducks migrate to avoid
cold weather.

DOWN FEATHERS
Female ducks pluck down
feathers from their breasts
and use them to line their
nests and cover the eggs
to keep them warm.

FEMALE

MALE

Short legs set well
back on body

MANDARIN DUCKS
These ducks live near ponds
and lakes surrounded by woods, and
nest in tree holes. The male is more
colorful than the female,
except when he molts his
feathers once a year.

CORNER CODING
Corners of habitat
pages are color
coded to remind
you which habitat
section you are in.

	TOWNS, CITIES, AND FARMLAND
	FOREST AND WOODLAND
	RAINFORESTS
	RIVERS, LAKES, AND SWAMPS
	SEAS, CLIFFS, AND SHORES
	DESERTS, SCRUB, AND GRASSLANDS
	MOUNTAINS AND MOORLAND
	POLAR AND TUNDRA REGIONS

HEADING
This describes the
subject of the page. This
page is about
ducks. If a subject
continues over
several pages, the
same heading applies.

INTRODUCTION
This provides a clear,
general overview of the
subject. After reading
this, you should have
an idea what the pages
are about.

CAPTIONS AND
ANNOTATIONS
Each illustration has a
caption. Annotations, in
italics, point out features
of an illustration and
usually have leader lines.

Running Heads

These remind you which section you are in. The top of the left-hand page gives the section name. The right-hand page gives the subject. This page on ducks is in the Rivers, Lakes, and Swamps section.

Fact Boxes

Many pages have fact boxes. These contain at-a-glance information about the subject. This fact box gives details such as the types of eggs and nests ducks have, and the food they eat.

Size Indicators

These show a bird next to a hand, or a human figure. The hand represents 7½ in (19 cm); the figure represents 6 ft (1.8 m).

Size indicator   Running head   Fact box

WOOD DUCK
Found in North America, wood ducks are related to Asian mandarin ducks. The females look after the nest, eggs, and ducklings on their own.

The ducklings swim soon after hatching

DIVING DUCKS
These ducks have plumper, rounder bodies than ducks that feed on the surface. Diving ducks, such as this pochard, can stay underwater for 30 seconds or more.

DUCK FACTS
• Family: Anatidae includes ducks, swans, and geese
• About 150 species
• Diurnal
• BILLBUILDERS
• Eat water plants and small water animals
• Habitat: ponds, lakes, rivers, or the sea
• Size: built size
• Eggs: white or pale

PLUMED WHISTLING-DUCK
Whistling-ducks live in the tropics and look more like geese than ducks. They feed mainly on the surface.

Webbed feet used like paddles for swimming

MALLARD
Mallards feed on the surface of the water or upend themselves to reach plant and animal food a little way below the surface. Mallards are the ancestors of most domestic ducks.

Wide, flat bill to sift food out of water

Label   Annotation

Labels

For extra clarity, some pictures have labels. They may give extra information, or identify a picture when it is not obvious from the text what it is.

Reference Section

The reference section pages are yellow and appear at the back of the book. On these, you will find useful facts, figures, and charts. These pages give bird records, such as the biggest and smallest birds, and the fastest flier and runner.

BIRD RECORDS
BIRDS HAVE DEVELOPED some remarkable adaptations in size, movement, appearance, and nesting behavior. The following examples are some of the more astonishing record breakers.

Index

There are two indexes at the back of the book – a subject index, and a scientific name index. The subject index lists every subject alphabetically. The scientific name index lists the scientific names of all the birds in the book.

9

INTRODUCTION TO BIRDS

WHAT IS A BIRD?

BIRDS ARE DIFFERENT from all the other animals in the world because they have feathers – at least a thousand of them. They also have two wings, a strong bill, no teeth, scaly legs and feet, and three or four toes with claws on the end. Most birds can fly and they are the largest, fastest, and most powerful flying animals. Like us, birds breathe air, have a skeleton inside their bodies, and are warm-blooded. Unlike us, birds lay eggs.

JUVENILE STARLING FEATHER

ADULT STARLING FEATHER

FEATHERS
Birds' feathers are light, yet strong and flexible. The feathers of young birds are often a different color from those of the adults.

STARLING EGGS

EGGS
A bird's egg is a survival capsule which protects and nourishes a baby bird while it develops inside. When the bird is ready to hatch, it has to force its way out.

Secondary flight feathers

Primary flight feathers

Rump

Uppertail coverts

Undertail coverts

Wing coverts

Ankle

Tail

EUROPEAN STARLING

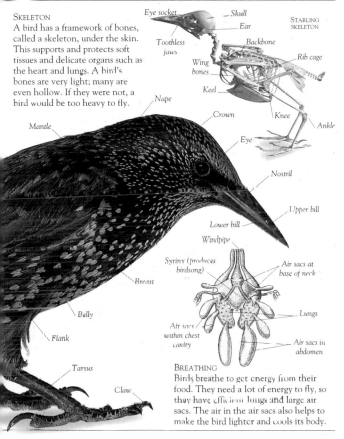

SKELETON

A bird has a framework of bones, called a skeleton, under the skin. This supports and protects soft tissues and delicate organs such as the heart and lungs. A bird's bones are very light; many are even hollow. If they were not, a bird would be too heavy to fly.

STARLING SKELETON

Eye socket

Skull

Ear

Toothless jaws

Backbone

Wing bones

Rib cage

Keel

Nape

Crown

Knee

Ankle

Mantle

Eye

Nostril

Upper bill

Lower bill

Windpipe

Syrinx (produces birdsong)

Air sacs at base of neck

Breast

Lungs

Belly

Air sacs within chest cavity

Air sacs in abdomen

Flank

Tarsus

BREATHING

Birds breathe to get energy from their food. They need a lot of energy to fly, so they have efficient lungs and large air sacs. The air in the air sacs also helps to make the bird lighter and cools its body.

Claw

Types of birds

The huge variety of birds alive today – over 9,000 species – evolved from reptilelike creatures that climbed trees about 150 million years ago. Reptile scales developed into bird feathers, although there are still scales on a bird's legs. Now, there are birds of all shapes and sizes, from huge ostriches to tiny wrens. Some of the main types of birds are shown here.

PIGEON

PIGEONS
Most pigeons and doves have rather small heads, plump bodies, dense, soft feathers, and a powerful straight flight. They live all over the world.

ARCHAEOPTERYX
The first bird we know of lived about 150 million years ago. It is called *Archaeopteryx*, meaning ancient wing. It had feathers, but could not fly well.

ANCIENT BIRD FACTS
• Birds may be living descendants of the dinosaurs.
• *Archaeopteryx* had teeth.
• The first flying bird was a ternlike seabird called *Ichthyornis*.
• The heaviest bird, *Dromornis stirtoni*, was four times heavier than an ostrich.

ZEBRA FINCHES

PERCHING BIRDS
Over half of the birds alive today are perching landbirds. Most are strong fliers and many sing well.

PARROTS
Colorful, noisy, tree-living birds of the tropics, parrots have powerful, hooked bills.

DUCKS
These are broad-bodied waterbirds with a wide, flat bill, webbed feet, and short legs set well back on the body.

WOOD DUCK

RED AND GREEN MACAW

KING PENGUIN

GOLDEN EAGLE

PENGUINS
These flightless seabirds of the Southern Hemisphere have wings like flippers.

EAGLES
Powerful birds of prey, eagles have broad, rounded wings, strong talons, and a hooked bill.

JUVENILE BLACK-HEADED GULL

GULLS
These sturdy seabirds have a heavy bill, long, pointed wings, and webbed feet.

Bird senses

Birds rely mainly on their eyes and ears to find food or a mate, to fly, and to escape from danger. Their eyes are so large that there is not much room for them to move in the skull. Instead, birds have a flexible neck and move their whole head to see things. Most birds have a poor sense of smell.

SIGHT
A bird's huge eyes are often as big as its brain. Much of the brain deals with the information picked up by the eyes. Like us, birds see in color, but many have far better eyesight than we have.

Large eyes to spot danger coming

PIED AVOCET

The avocet uses its sense of touch to catch small water creatures.

TOUCH
Some birds, such as the avocet, have a well-developed sense of touch in the tongue and bill tip. Nightjars have bristles around their broad bills to help them sweep moths into their mouths as they fly at night.

WOODCOCK EYES

To watch for danger, woodcocks have eyes on the side of their head. This helps them to see all around, but there are two blind spots behind and in front of the head.

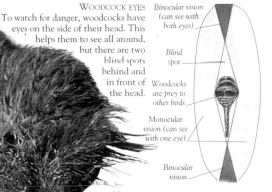

Binocular vision (can see with both eyes)

Blind spot

Woodcocks are prey to other birds

Monocular vision (can see with one eye)

Binocular vision

HEARING

Birds hear a higher frequency of sound – more sounds per second – than we can. Good hearing is very important to birds that hunt in the dark, but all birds need to hear other birds singing so that they can communicate.

A bird breathes and smells through two openings in its bill.

BROWN KIWI

SMELL

Most birds seem to have a poor sense of smell, but there are a few exceptions. The kiwi smells food with nostrils at the tip of its long bill. The vultures of the Americas can detect the smell of rotting dead animals from some distance. Some seabirds can pick up scents carried by the wind.

FEATHERS

A BIRD'S BODY is almost completely covered with feathers, although some birds have bare legs. Feathers keep the bird warm, give it shape, color, and pattern, and help most birds to fly. Some birds have special display feathers. Feathers carry out many important jobs, so they need to be kept in good condition.

What is a feather?

There are three main types of feather – flight, body, and down. Feathers grow out of pits or follicles in a bird's skin, like the hairs all over our bodies. They can be easily repaired because of the way the parts of the feather hook together.

Web or vane

Smooth, curved shape for flight

Shaft or rachis

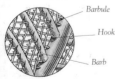

Barbule

Hook

Barb

BARBS AND BARBULES
Each side of a feather consists of parallel barbs, held in place by tiny hooks on side branches called barbules. There are many thousands of barbules on a flight feather.

MACAW FLIGHT FEATHER

FEATHER STRUCTURE
Feathers have a central shaft with a web or vane on either side. They are made of a strong, flexible material called keratin, which also forms our hair and nails.

FLIGHT FEATHERS

Found in the wings and tail, flight feathers provide a large area to push the bird through the air. Their special airfoil shape lifts the bird in the air, and controls the way it twists and turns in flight.

PEACOCK DOWN FEATHER

Short shaft

DOWN FEATHERS

The soft down feathers trap warm air next to the body and are very important in young birds. The barbs are long and soft and the barbules do not hook together so the feather stays fluffy.

REGENT PARROT FLIGHT FEATHER

Long shaft

AFRICAN GRAY PARROT BODY FEATHER

Inner fluffy part to keep bird warm

Quill

BODY FEATHERS

Overlapping like tiles on a roof, body feathers act as a weatherproof jacket. The inner part has softer barbs and the barbules have no hooks.

FEATHER FACTS

• Swans have 25,000 feathers, sparrows 3,500, and hummingbirds less than 1,000.

• The male crested argus pheasant has the largest tail feathers at 5¼ ft (173cm) long, 5in (13cm) wide.

• Feathers evolved from reptile scales.

• Grebes eat their feathers to help digestion.

Feather color

The colors of bird feathers are produced in two ways.
One is by chemical pigments laid down in the feather
when it is being formed. The other is by the structure
of feathers and the way they reflect light. Bird colors
help individuals of the same species to recognize each
other. They also help birds attract a mate, threaten a
rival, or camouflage themselves.

SHINING COLORS
Peacock feathers are iridescent –
they change colors as they move.
This is probably caused by a
mixture of pigments and
reflection of the light.

*Male peacock
uses his colorful
feathers in a
courtship display.*

FLAMINGO
FEATHERS

FOOD COLOR
The color of flamingo
feathers comes from a
pink pigment in the
shrimps and other small
water creatures which the
birds sieve from the water.

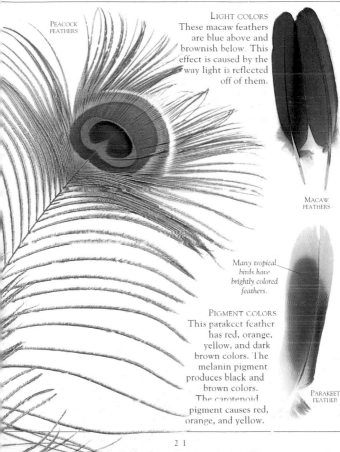

PEACOCK
FEATHERS

LIGHT COLORS
These macaw feathers
are blue above and
brownish below. This
effect is caused by the
way light is reflected
off of them.

MACAW
FEATHERS

*Many tropical
birds have
brightly colored
feathers.*

PIGMENT COLORS
This parakeet feather
has red, orange,
yellow, and dark
brown colors. The
melanin pigment
produces black and
brown colors.
The carotenoid
pigment causes red,
orange, and yellow.

PARAKEET
FEATHER

Looking after feathers

Birds must take great care of their feathers
and spend a few hours each day
cleaning their plumage.
They use the bill to
pull ruffled feathers
into shape, and
may also take
water or dust
baths. Many
birds spread
an oily liquid
over their
feathers to
keep them
waterproof.

YELLOW
CANARY
PREENING

PREENING
To preen its feathers, a bird draws
each one carefully through its bill.
This fits the barbs and barbules back
into place – like pulling up a zipper –
and cleans and smooths the feathers.
Preening also removes parasites, such
as feather lice, which live on feathers
and eat them.

*Most birds use
their feet to
preen their head
feathers.*

*The oil used for preening
comes from a special
gland at the base of the
tail, on the rump.*

BIRD BATH

Many birds, like the blue tit below, bathe in water. They clean their feathers and skin, and get ready for preening. Most birds bathe and preen regularly. Some also take dust baths, perhaps to get rid of parasites.

NEW FEATHERS

A new feather is rolled up as a cylinder inside a thin, horny sheath. When it is fully developed, the sheath splits open and flakes away. The feather can then unroll and begin to grow to its full length.

Emerging adult feather

Fully grown tail feather

Young penguins lose their fluffy feathers.

MOLTING KING PENGUINS

ADULT KESTREL FEATHER

Horny sheath

YOUNG KESTREL FEATHER

GROWING FEATHERS

At least once a year, most birds molt their feathers and new feathers grow to replace old ones. Molting allows birds to replace worn or damaged feathers, and to change color as they grow up or the seasons change.

HOW BIRDS MOVE

TO FIND FOOD and escape danger, birds walk, run, hop, swim, and wade. Most birds can also fly. They have light bones, powerful flight muscles, and an efficient respiratory system. A few birds cannot fly, but some of these flightless birds run very fast.

Flight

Most birds fly by flapping their wings up and down. As the wings beat down, they push the air back, making the bird move forward.

LIFT
Birds have curved wings covered with feathers to push and steer them through the air. The inner part of a bird's wing can stay still to provide lift.

TAKEOFF
A heavy bird, such as a swan, has to run while flapping its wings to get enough lift for take-off. Smaller birds take off by jumping into the air and then flapping their wings to create lift.

TAWNY OWL

COMING IN TO LAND

To land, birds slow down in midair, then drop gently to the ground, onto a perch, or the surface of the water, spreading out their wings and tail like brakes. Heavy birds land into the wind to help slow themselves down.

Strong legs to absorb impact of landing

Wings and tail spread to increase air resistance and drag

CURVED WINGS

A bird's wing is an airfoil shape – curved on top and slightly hollow underneath. The air flows faster over the top, creating low air pressure, while air pressure underneath stays much the same. The difference in pressure produces lift.

BLUE-AND-WHITE FLYCATCHER

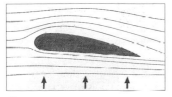

Fingerlike feathers to push and steer through the air

FLIGHT FACTS

• Common swifts may stay in the air for three years at a time without landing.

• Some hummingbirds beat their wings up to 90 times a second.

• Swans have been recorded flying as high as 29,500 ft (8,230 m).

• Peregrine falcons can reach speeds of 112 mph (180 km/h) when diving after prey.

MUTE SWAN

Neck stretched out and feet tucked up to streamline bird's body

Flight patterns

Different kinds of birds have differently shaped wings which they flap in patterns that suit their lifestyle. To save energy, some birds like gulls and vultures soar on rising air, while smaller birds glide between flaps of the wings. Ducks and other heavy birds flap their wings all the time they are in the air. A few, such as hummingbirds and kestrels, can hover in one spot.

Feathers spread apart on upstroke for air to slip through wing

UP AND DOWN FLIGHT
Small birds, like this red-tailed minla, have a bouncing, undulating flight. Bigger birds such as cranes, ducks, and geese tend to fly in straight lines.

RED-TAILED MINLA

Eagles thermaling

Hot air rising

Seabirds have powerful flight muscles.

GLIDING IN A THERMAL

GLIDING AND SOARING
Seabirds glide upward on air currents rising from waves or over cliffs. Large birds of prey, such as eagles or vultures, also use natural currents of rising hot air to lift them higher. These currents are called thermals.

HOVERING

Hummingbirds can hover,
move straight up or down, and
even fly backward. They do this by
turning each wing in a circle, and using
up and down wingbeats for extra power.

HUMMINGBIRD

*Unlike other birds,
hummingbirds have rigid
wings with a swivel joint at
the shoulder.*

*Between flaps,
wings fold against
body so bird can
glide and rest*

*Feathers closed
together on downstroke
to push against the air*

*Tail used for steering
and changing direction*

GLIDING
HERRING GULL

*Long, narrow wings
for gliding*

*Feathers hug the
body, creating a
streamlined shape so air
can flow past more easily.*

WING SHAPE

The size and shape of wings give
clues to how a bird lives and helps
with identification, especially if
the bird is high in the sky.

*Long and wide for soaring –
vultures and some hawks*

*Long and narrow for gliding –
fulmars and albatrosses*

*Wide and rounded for short,
fast flight – pheasants*

*Narrow and pointed for fast
flight – swallows and swifts*

CASSOWARY
AND CHICK

Flightless birds

A few birds do not fly at all. Some of
them swim or run so well that they do
not need to fly. Many flightless birds,
such as ostriches, rheas, or emus, are
very large birds that can run faster than
their enemies, or can win a fight so
easily that they do not need to fly away.
Other flightless birds live on remote
islands where there are few enemies
from which they need to escape.

DEFENSE
With powerful legs and
daggerlike claws, birds such
as cassowaries do not need
to fly away. Cassowaries
even attack people, lashing
out with strong feet and
sharp nails.

FLIGHTLESS
CORMORANT

FLIGHTLESS FACTS

• The heaviest bird of
all time was *Dromornis
stirtoni*, a flightless bird
that died out about
25,000 years ago.

• Ostriches are nearly
seven times too heavy to
fly. They have the
biggest legs of any bird,
over 4 ft (1.2 m) long.

• The Inaccessible
Island rail is the world's
smallest flightless bird,
about the size of a chick.

WINGS
Flightless birds usually have
small, weak wings which are
not strong enough for flight.
The flightless cormorant
uses its wings to help it
balance on land.

BIRDS IN DANGER
Many flightless birds, such as
this kakapo, are threatened
by the cats and rats
introduced to their
island homes by
settlers. Kakapos
are too heavy to fly.

KAKAPO

GREATER
RHEA

FAST RUNNERS

Running away from danger can be just as good as
flying. Rheas can sprint faster than a horse, reaching
speeds of 31 mph (50 km/h), and are also good
swimmers. Rheas are related to ostriches and emus
and follow a similar lifestyle, but they live on the
South American grasslands, rather than on the
grasslands of Africa or Australia.

*Fluffy wings
used for display,
not flight*

*Long neck to
see over tall
grasses*

HUMBOLDT
PENGUIN

FAST SWIMMERS

Penguins are well
suited to their life
in the sea – they are
even a different
shape from most
birds. They use their
wings as flippers
for swimming, while
their feet and tail
steer like a rudder.

*Large leg
muscles
provide power
for running*

*Three strong toes
on each foot for
defense and for
running fast*

LEGS AND FEET

BIRDS USE their legs and feet for preening their feathers, as well as for moving around. The size and shape of their feet depends on where they live and how they feed.

Three toes point forward and one back

Stringlike tendons

PERCHING
Birds that perch can sleep without falling off a branch. They bend their legs, pulling the tendons tight and drawing in the toes. This locks their feet tightly around the perch.

TAWNY OWL TALON

TALONS
Birds of prey, such as owls and eagles, have strong, sharp, curved claws called talons. They use these to catch and carry their prey.

Long toes are spread wide

WATTLED JACANA

Scaly skin along each toe

WIDE TOES
Some water birds, such as coots, have lobes of skin on each toe. These push aside the water for faster swimming and help to stop the coot from sinking into mud.

COOT TOES

LONG TOES
Jacanas, or lily trotters, have very long, thin toes. These spread the weight of the bird over a bigger area so it can "trot" across lily pads on the ponds and lakes where it lives.

SPEED
Ostriches have long legs and strong toes to run at speeds of up to 60 mph (97.5 km/h). They have only two toes on each foot; most birds have three or four.

BLUE FRONTED PARROT

WEBBED FEET
Waterbirds, such as ducks, gulls, and flamingos, have webs of skin between their toes. The webs work like paddles when the bird is in water. They are also useful when the bird is walking on soft, marshy ground.

GRIPPING TOES
The two outer toes of a parrot's foot point backward, and the two inner toes point forward. This gives parrots a very powerful grip for climbing through the trees. It also allows them to hold food up to the bill.

Two toes forward, two toes back

FLAMINGO

COLLARED
SUNBIRD SIPPING
NECTAR

FOOD AND FEEDING

BIRDS SPEND MUCH of their time
finding food, whether pecking at
berries and nuts, or snapping up fish or
small mammals. They rely mainly on their
eyes and ears to find food, and their bill or
claws to catch it. A few birds steal their food
from other birds. Some birds eat plants; others
eat animals or have a mixed diet.

Hunting and fishing

Meat-eating birds usually catch weak
or unfit prey. They may lie in wait to
ambush their quarry, or chase after it
through air or water. Most of these
birds hunt by day; a few, such as
owls, hunt at night.

GREAT WHITE
PELICAN

GOLDEN
EAGLE

BIRDS OF PREY
Most birds of
prey, such as this
golden eagle, soar
high in the sky to
search for food,
then swoop down to
seize and crush prey in
their sharp talons. However, nine out
of ten attacks are unsuccessful and the
prey manages to escape.

*A pelican's bill can
hold more food than
its stomach.*

UMBRELLA FISHING
Some birds have developed their own special techniques for catching food. The black heron shades the water with its wings. This cuts out reflections and makes it easier for the bird to see fish.

SNAKE HUNTERS
Secretary birds are unusual because they search for their prey mainly on foot. They have tough scales on their legs for protection from snakebites. They pin prey to the ground with sharp claws.

Great white pelicans eat about 2 ½ lb (1.2 kg) of fish a day.

Sharp, hooked bill to pull and tear at food

EGYPTIAN VULTURE

FISHING IN GROUPS
Great white pelicans usually fish in groups. The birds gather in a circle on the water, lifting their wings and plunging their bills into the water to drive the fish into the middle of the circle. Then they scoop up the fish.

USING TOOLS
A few birds use tools to find and obtain their food. Egyptian vultures throw or drop stones onto ostrich eggs to break open the thick shells.

What birds eat

Birds have healthy appetites. They need to eat large amounts of food to give them enough energy to fly, keep warm, build nests, and lay eggs. Some birds eat only one kind of food, while others, such as starlings, crows, and jays, eat almost anything. Vultures eat carcasses, the dead bodies of animals.

HELMET BIRD

MICROSCOPIC SEAFOOD
A drop of seawater teems with tiny organisms such as diatoms, plankton, and crab larvae. This plankton floats about the oceans and is a vital part of the diet of many seabirds.

ACORN

SEEDS

RASPBERRY

HIBISCUS FLOWER

FLOWERS, FRUITS, AND SEEDS
For hummingbirds, the sweet liquid called nectar produced by flowers is a high-energy food. Many birds eat the fruits and seeds that develop when the flowers are pollinated.

GRASS

CABBAGE LEAF

CONIFER

GRASS AND LEAVES
A few birds, like geese, ducks, and grouse, eat grass and leaves. These can be hard to digest and poor in nutrients, so the birds have to eat a lot of this sort of food to get the energy they need.

GROUND BEETLE

FLY

GRASSHOPPER

CRAB

SNAIL

COCKLE

EARTHWORM

INSECTS
Adult insects are more abundant in warmer weather, but caterpillars and grubs survive colder periods buried in soil or under bark. Insects are a body-building food, vital for young birds.

INVERTEBRATES
Invertebrates such as crabs and shellfish are an important source of food on the seashore, where there are few insects. Garden and woodland birds, such as thrushes, eat juicy earthworms.

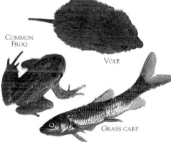

COMMON FROG

VOLE

GRASS CARP

NEST AND YOUNG

VERTEBRATES
Birds that feed on vertebrates (animals with backbones) have to work hard for meals. The animals they hunt can run, swim, or slither away, and often succeed in escaping.

EGGS AND YOUNG
Some birds eat the eggs and helpless young of other birds. For example, skuas pounce on puffin and penguin chicks, and magpies often take eggs and young birds from the nest.

Bird bills

A bird uses its bill like a hand to carry out all sorts of tasks, from catching and holding food to preening its feathers and building a nest. Parrots also use their bills to help them climb. The size and shape of a bird's bill depends mainly on what it eats and where it finds its food.

YELLOW-CROWNED PARROT

FLAMINGO

FRUIT-AND-NUT EATERS
A parrot's bill deals with two different kinds of food. The hook at the tip pulls out the soft parts of fruit, while the strong nutcracker at the base opens seeds. Parrots use their feet to hold food.

A flamingo dips its bill in the shallow water upside-down

Bee-eaters beat stinging insects against a branch to get rid of the stings.

WHITE-THROATED BEE-EATER

FILTER-FEEDER
The flamingo has a very special bill. Sievelike edges on the top bill filter out tiny plants, shrimps, and other invertebrates from the water. The bottom bill and the tongue move up and down to pump water through comblike fringes on the sides of the top bill.

INSECT EATERS
Birds that feed on insects have thin, pointed bills to probe under bark and stones. Birds that eat flying insects have wide, gaping bills to scoop them up as they fly.

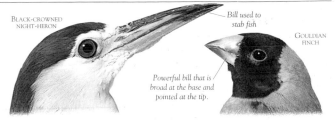

BLACK-CROWNED
NIGHT-HERON

Bill used to
stab fish

GOULDIAN
FINCH

Powerful bill that is
broad at the base and
pointed at the tip.

FISH EATERS

A dagger-shaped bill is characteristic of
fish-eating birds, such as herons. Others,
such as ospreys, have a hooked bill with
which to tear the fish into pieces.

SEED EATERS

To crack open seeds, seed-eating birds
such as finches have pyramid-shaped
bills. The hawfinch's bill is so strong it
can even crush cherry stones.

SCARLET-CHESTED
SUNBIRD

Flaps over
nostrils keep out
flower pollen

NECTAR EATERS

Nearly one-fifth of all the
world's birds feed on nectar.
Sunbirds and hummingbirds
push their needlelike bills into
flowers and lick up the sweet nectar.

Powerful
hooked bill to
tear up food

GOLDEN
EAGLE

MEAT EATERS

Often called birds of prey, these include
eagles, owls, and falcons. They use their
bills to pull apart animals they kill into
bite-sized chunks. Owls swallow small
animals, such as voles and mice, whole.

COURTSHIP

BEFORE MATING, male birds usually court the females. Some males grow more colorful or elaborate feathers for the breeding season. They may give singing or dancing displays. Some show off nest-building or hunting skills.

YELLOW-
THROATED
LAUGHING
THRUSH

Laughing thrushes make loud, cackling sounds.

TERRITORY
Many birds nest in an area, or territory, which has enough food for their young when they hatch out. Male birds sing in their territory to attract a mate and keep away other males.

MALE
PIN-TAILED
WHYDAH

Female bird duller, with short tail

MALES AND FEMALES
Male and female birds of the same species often look different. The male is usually more colorful, but the dull colors of the female help camouflage her on the nest.

Long tail feathers used in display flight to impress females

FEMALE
PIN-TAILED
WHYDAH

MALE
PEACOCK

*Male's long
feathers make
flight difficult*

DISPLAY
The male
peacock erects his
long, colorful feathers
in a shimmering fan to
impress a female. After the
breeding season, the long tail
feathers fall out.

*The "eyes"
may hypnotize
the female.*

JAPANESE
CRANES

DANCING
Some birds dance together
before they mate. Cranes jump
up and down in the air with
their partners. Great crested
grebes perform a series of
dances, including head-shaking.

39

NESTS AND EGGS

All birds lay eggs and most build nests to keep eggs and young safe and warm. Birds know instinctively how to build a nest, and female birds usually do most of the work. Nests vary from a shallow scrape in the ground and simple cup shapes, to more elaborate constructions.

Building a nest

NEST BOX

Birds use a wide range of nesting materials and may make hundreds of trips to collect material. Nest materials must both support the nest and keep the young warm. Nest boxes encourage birds to nest in gardens or woods with few natural tree holes.

WAGTAIL NEST

PEBBLE NEST
Oystercatchers lay their eggs in a shallow dip, or scrape, on the shoreline. Their eggs are difficult to see among the pebbles.

TWIGS
Most hedgerow and woodland birds use twigs and sticks to support their nests since these are readily available.

FEATHERS
Birds use feathers as a warm lining for a nest. Hundreds of feathers line a long-tailed tit's nest.

To make the cup shape, birds turn around and around.

Moss

Moss traps warm air in the nest and stops heat loss. It helps to keep both eggs and young birds warm.

String

Birds often collect household materials when nest building. Pieces of string have been found in many nests.

Mud

Some nests are lined with wet mud mixed with saliva and droppings. When it dries, it forms a hard and strong lining.

Mud nest

Swallows and martins collect mud with their bills, and build nests with pieces of mud stuck together with saliva.

Woodpeckers have chisel-like bills.

Tree nest

Woodpeckers dig nest holes in rotten trees with their strong beaks. Many other birds use existing tree holes. The nests inside the holes are usually lined with grass or feathers.

House martin nest

Grass

Grass is a flexible nest material. It is used by many birds because it is easy to weave into differently shaped nests.

Unusual nests

From woven purses and saliva cups to mud ovens and compost heaps, some birds' nests are quite unusual, while others are very elaborate. They may be a strange shape, such as the trumpetlike weaverbird nests, or made with unusual materials, such as the birds' own saliva.

PENDULINE-TIT NEST

Strong and lightweight basket

False entrance

WOVEN NEST
A male West African weaver knotted grasses to weave this nest. The entrance tunnel stops snakes and other enemies from getting inside.

PURSE NEST
The penduline-tit weaves a hanging nest from grasses, leaves, and moss. A false entrance leads to an empty chamber and dead end.

THATCHED COTTAGE
Each colony of the social weaverbirds of South Africa builds a huge "haystack" that is up to 13 ft (4 m) deep and 24 ft (7.2 m) across. Up to 300 pairs then build their nests under the protection of this thatched roof.

WEAVER NEST

NEST FACTS

• The biggest tree nest ever found belonged to a bald eagle. It was 9½ ft (2.9 m) wide and 20 ft (6 m) deep.

• A bee hummingbird's nest is no bigger than a thimble.

• A malleefowl's nest is a "compost heap" of rotting vegetation.

• A hamerkop nest may consist of over 10,000 sticks.

BASKET NEST

Reed warblers join their nest to several reed stems. This helps to hold the nest steady as the wind blows. The nest is made from grass, reed fibers, and feathers.

Nest is joined to reeds

REED WARBLER NEST

TAILORBIRD NEST

SEWING BIRD

The tailorbird sews a pocket of leaves to support its nest. Its sharp bill makes a row of holes along the edges of the leaves. Then the bird pulls spider or insect silk or plant material through the holes to stitch the leaves.

NORTHERN ORIOLE NEST

STRING NEST

Many birds that nest near people make use of artificial materials. This northern oriole has used pieces of string in its baglike nest, and has even joined the nest to a twig with string.

All kinds of eggs

Like dinosaurs and other reptiles, birds lay eggs in which the embryos grow and are nourished. Some birds lay one large clutch (set of eggs) in a season, while others lay several smaller clutches. Some birds, such as snowy owls, lay extra clutches if there is plenty of food. No two eggs have exactly the same markings. The color and shape depend on where the eggs are laid and how much camouflage they need.

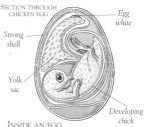

SECTION THROUGH CHICKEN EGG

Egg white

Strong shell

Yolk sac

Developing chick

INSIDE AN EGG
A bird's egg contains a developing bird – an embryo – plus a store of food and a supply of air. Pores in the shell allow air to pass through from outside. The egg white supplies proteins, water, and vitamins.

EGG FACTS

• One ostrich egg has the same volume as 24 hens' eggs.

• Cuckoos can lay eggs in a few seconds; some birds take 1-3 minutes.

• Nearly 80 species of birds lay eggs in the nests of other species.

• Gray partridges lay the largest clutches – up to 16 eggs.

• Most small eggs take under an hour to hatch.

BARN OWL EGG

CURLEW EGG

WHITE EGGS
Birds that nest in holes or burrows, such as owls or kingfishers, usually lay white eggs. They do not need to be camouflaged because they are hidden.

SPECKLED EGGS
Birds that nest in the open, where there is little cover, usually lay patterned eggs. The camouflage colors hide the eggs from predators.

PALE EGG

SPECKLED EGG

DARK EGG
EGG

DISGUISE
Female cuckoos lay their eggs in the nests of other birds such as catbirds, robins, wrens, or meadow pipits. The foster parents raise the cuckoo chick as their own. The cuckoo's egg often looks similar to those of the foster parents.

COLORS IN A CLUTCH
The three eggs above were laid by a single snipe but come from different clutches. In one clutch, the eggs usually look similar.

CUCKOO
EGG

Pear shape to roll in a circle

EURASIAN
ROBIN EGGS

BIG AND SMALL
Ostriches lay the largest eggs of any living bird. Each egg weighs about 3½ lb (1.7 kg), and is as long as an adult human's hand. Hummingbirds' eggs, however, are only as big as peas.

PATTERNS
Common murre eggs show a variety of patterns and colors, possibly to help parent birds recognize them. The pear shape stops it from rolling off cliff ledges.

HUMMINGBIRD
EGGS

OSTRICH EGG

BIRTH AND GROWTH

PARENT BIRDS SIT on their eggs to keep them warm so that the chicks inside can develop properly. This is called incubation. After the chicks hatch, the parents work hard feeding the chicks, keeping them warm and clean, and protecting them from enemies.

Egg to chick

In order to incubate, most birds develop patches of bare skin, brood patches, to let body warmth through

SWAN INCUBATING EGGS IN NEST

to the eggs. Small birds incubate for about two weeks, eagles for five to seven weeks, and albatrosses for up to 11 weeks. Some baby birds are helpless when they hatch. Others can soon run around.

First the chick pecks at shell to make a hole

Then chick cuts a circle

Chick pushes to widen crack

HATCHING
To break out of its shell, a baby bird chips away with a pointed "egg tooth" on top of its bill. This egg tooth disappears soon after hatching. Some chicks, such as quail, can walk about immediately after hatching out of their shells.

Helpless young are usually born in a nest.

BLUE TIT NEST

HELPLESS CHICKS

Birds born naked, blind, and feeble are called altricial. They grow at a very fast rate, often eating their own weight each day. Songbirds, such as thrushes and chaffinches, are born like this.

INDEPENDENT CHICKS

Some chicks are born with feathers, and are able to see and run soon after hatching. They are called precocial. Ducks, geese, and terns are born like this.

Wet and bedraggled chick struggles free.

Dry and fluffy feathers

BLUE-SCALED QUAIL CHICK

Growing up

Baby birds take a few weeks or a few months to grow up. They all rely on their parents to keep them warm and out of danger, and most chicks are fed by their parents as well. Small birds may make hundreds of feeding trips in a day; larger birds only two or three. Chicks that are born helpless grow faster than chicks that hatch fluffy and alert.

EAGLE AND CHICKS

HEN AND CHICKS

BIRDS OF PREY
Eagles and other birds of prey tear up food for their chicks at first. As the chicks grow bigger, they learn to tear it up for themselves.

INDEPENDENT FEEDERS
Some baby birds, such as chicks, ducklings, and goslings, can feed themselves soon after hatching. At first, they peck at anything; then they watch their parents to find out what to eat.

PECKING SPOT
A herring gull chick pecks at a red spot on its parent's bill to make the parent cough up food. Herring gulls feed out at sea, so they swallow food rather than carry it long distances.

HERRING GULL

CRÈCHE OF YOUNG
KING PENGUINS

Young penguins huddle together for warmth and protection while their parents are away.

SAFETY IN NUMBERS

Young penguins cannot join their parents in the water until they have grown waterproof adult feathers. The parent birds leave them behind when they go to sea to feed. When they return, the adults cough up partly digested fish for the chicks, but there may be a wait of days or even weeks between meals.

JUVENILE
STARLING

A young starling takes off unsteadily for its first flight.

FIRST FLIGHT

Baby birds have to learn how to fly as quickly as possible to avoid predators and other dangers. They flap their wings while they are in the nest to exercise their muscles and make them strong. Taking off and landing is not easy — many young birds crash-land.

MIGRATION

NEARLY HALF the world's birds migrate
to find food and water, to nest, or to
avoid bad weather. They navigate by
instinct, but use familiar landmarks, the
Sun, Moon, and stars, and
the Earth's magnetic field to
find their way. Migration
journeys are often dangerous
for birds and use up a
lot of energy. Some
small birds double
their weight to
provide enough
fuel for traveling.

RED-BREASTED
GOOSE

NESTING
This goose is one of many
birds that migrate to arctic
tundra to nest in the brief
summer when there is plenty
of food available.

MIGRATION ROUTES

ARCTIC TERN
This is the champion bird migrant,
flying from the Arctic to Antarctica
and back each year. It spends
summer in both polar regions.

AMERICAN GOLDEN-PLOVER
This plover has the longest
migration of any land bird. It breeds
in northern Canada and flies to the
Argentinian pampas for the winter.

V-FORMATION

Flying in a V-shaped formation helps birds to
save energy on a long journey. The birds
following the leader fly in the slipstream of
the bird in front. When the leader
tires, another bird
takes over.

SNOW GEESE
MIGRATING

*Snow geese breed in
the arctic tundra and
migrate to the Gulf of
Mexico for the winter.*

MOUNTAIN MIGRATION

Some birds migrate short
distances. The Himalayan
monal, a pheasant, migrates up
and down the mountains with
the seasons, moving to warmer,
lower slopes in winter.

HIMALAYAN
MONAL
PHEASANTS

MIGRATION FACTS

• American golden-
plovers are fast
migrants, flying
2,050 miles (3,300 km)
in 35 hours.

• The ruby-throated
hummingbird travels
2,000 miles (3,200 km)
across the Americas

• Most migrating birds
fly below 300 ft (91 m).

SHORT-TAILED SHEARWATER

Between breeding seasons off
southern Australia, this bird flies
in a figure-eight route from Australia
to the North Pacific and back again.

GREATER WHITETHROAT

This small warbler breeds in Europe
in spring and summer, and then
migrates to Africa just south of the
Sahara Desert for the winter.

WHERE BIRDS LIVE

FROM BUSY CITIES to frozen polar regions, birds have adapted to a range of habitats on every continent. Where birds live depends on the food they eat and their nesting requirements, as well as their competitors and predators. In many parts of the world, people have had a destructive influence on the distribution of birds.

NORTH AMERICA

SOUTH AMERICA

SEAS, CLIFFS, AND SHORES
Marine habitats are a huge feeding ground for many birds. They nest on islands and continental shores.

DESERTS, SCRUB, AND GRASSLANDS
These dry, mainly hot habitats provide little shelter for birds. Food and water may be hard to find.

POLAR AND TUNDRA REGIONS
In the Antarctic, Arctic, and tundra, it is cold and windy. Birds breed there in summer.

RIVERS, LAKES, AND SWAMPS
Lakes and rivers are freshwater, while marshes and swamps are fresh- or saltwater.

FORESTS AND WOODLANDS
Conifers and broad-leaved trees grow in temperate climates where there is usually rain all year.

TOWNS, CITIES, AND FARMLAND
Birds that have adapted to live near people can take advantage of the extra food and the less severe climate.

MOUNTAINS AND MOORLANDS
Moorlands occur in cool, wet uplands. Mountains have a variety of habitats.

RAIN FORESTS
These are mostly hot, wet habitats near the Equator in the Americas, Africa, southeast Asia, and northeast Australia.

TOWNS, CITIES, AND FARMLAND

ABOUT THE HABITAT

BIRDS THAT HAVE LEARNED to live close to people can feast on the food we give them, or the garbage we throw away, as well as the weeds, flowers, insects, or farm crops around our homes. Birds that used to nest on cliffs or in caves, nest in buildings or under bridges, and woodland birds nest in hedgerows.

EURASIAN KESTREL

HUNTING BIRDS
Most birds of prey do not like living near people, but kestrels and sparrowhawks hunt along roadsides and in parks.

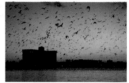

CITY BIRDS
Birds such as geese fly over cities on migration routes, or land to feed and roost in city parks. Starlings roost in city centers at night because it is warmer than the countryside.

HABITAT FACTS

• At night, a city is as much as 9°F (5°C) warmer than the surrounding countryside.

• Some starling roosts in cities may contain over one million birds.

• Of every 10 birds caught in the wild, only 1 reaches the pet shop alive.

• The African red-billed quelea is the world's worst agricultural bird pest.

CAGED BIRDS
Many people keep birds such as budgerigars, canaries, and parrots in cages. They like their colors, their company, and their songs. People breed birds to create colors never seen in the wild.

BLUE BUDGERIGAR

BARN
SWALLOW
FEEDING
YOUNG

NESTS IN BUILDINGS
Window ledges,
attics, barns, and even
chimney pots make ideal nesting places
for birds used to nesting on cliffs,
rocky hillsides, or trees. Swallows
used to nest in caves, but now
many nest inside buildings.

NESTS IN HEDGEROWS
Hedgerows are small strips of
woodland where birds such as
the song thrush can nest safely.
Birds roost and feed in hedgerows.
They are an important refuge in
open areas of crops and grass.

SONG THRUSH

SONG THRUSH NEST

HOMES AND STREETS

MANY BIRDS HAVE LOST their natural fear of people and live near our homes and in our cities, despite all the noise and pollution. These urban birds change their diet or the places they nest to take advantage of our leftover food scraps, the artificial habitats we build, and the warm climates we create.

HOUSE SPARROW
By following people from country to country, the fearless house sparrow has spread from Europe and Asia over two-thirds of the world's land surface. It nests in buildings close to people.

This is a male with a gray crown and black bib.

The house sparrow is friendly and intelligent.

CAGED BIRDS
Every year, people take thousands of birds from the wild, often illegally. This has critically reduced the numbers of some wild birds, especially parrots.

WHITE STORKS
In many parts of Europe, white storks are believed to bring good luck. They often nest on roofs, and people may put up platforms to encourage them.

Red streak below eye and upright black crest

HOUSE CROW

The aggressive house crow is always ready to grasp a tasty morsel of food. It lives near busy towns and small villages in India, as well as in other parts of Asia, often swarming in large, busy groups.

Likes to perch on a high branch to sing

RED-WHISKERED BULBUL

The inquisitive red-whiskered bulbul is not frightened of people and is a common species around the villages of Asia. It has a pleasant and varied song and is often kept as a pet.

Pigeons are tame enough to be fed by hand.

PIGEON

The city pigeons of today are descended from the wild rock doves that people originally kept for food and, later, for racing. Pigeons are the only bird group to feed their young with a secretion called pigeon's milk.

City pigeons even travel on subways.

PARKS AND GARDENS

FROM TREES AND FLOWERBEDS to grassy lawns and garden ponds, parks and gardens contain a great variety of habitats for birds. People put up feeding tables, birdbaths, and nesting boxes to encourage birds to live near houses. Unfortunately, pets such as cats often catch and kill garden birds.

BLACK-BILLED MAGPIE
This adaptable magpie visits surburban gardens. It eats a range of food, especially insects and small rodents, but also steals eggs and young from the nests of other birds.

Pale gray border

Orange breast and face typical of robins

EUROPEAN ROBIN
These birds are aggressive. Males often set up territories in gardens and sing loudly to keep away other male robins. In winter, both males and females defend feeding territories.

BLUE TITS

These bold, lively birds often visit gardens in winter to feed on nuts, seeds, and leftover food scraps put out by people. They can easily land on nut feeders and often use the nest boxes that people build and put up for them.

Blue tits are agile, acrobatic birds.

Cone-shaped bill typical of a seed eater

WATERFOWL IN PARKS

The artificial lakes in parks make a welcome feeding, resting, and nesting area for swans, ducks, and grebes. Islands in the middle of lakes provide safe nesting places.

NORTHERN CARDINAL

These cardinals are frequent visitors to feeders in the backyards of North America. They often move around in pairs or family groups to feed on seeds that people leave out for them.

SUPERB STARLING

A common visitor to campsites and hotels in East Africa, the superb starling is a tame bird, not frightened of people. It feeds mainly on the ground, pecking up seeds, fruit, and insects.

FIELDS AND HEDGEROWS

FARMLAND HAS TAKEN the place of woodlands, grasslands, and wetlands, but some birds have adapted to this habitat. They feed on the crops and nest in the animal pastures, hedges, orchards, and farm buildings. However, numbers of farmland birds have been reduced by the removal of hedgerows and the use of poisonous pesticides.

EUROPEAN GOLDFINCH
Flocks of goldfinches feed on weeds along the edges of fields. They are light enough to perch on thistle heads and eat the seeds.

FOLLOWING THE PLOW
Large flocks of birds, such as black-headed gulls, often follow a tractor plowing a field. The birds feed on the insects and other invertebrates, such as worms, exposed by the plow.

Gulls feed on newly plowed land.

HOOPOE
In the Mediterranean the weeds and grasses under the olive groves teem with invertebrates. Hoopoes probe the ground with long curved bills for worms and insects.

RING-NECKED PHEASANT
The female pheasant may nest in hedgerows, making a shallow scrape in the ground in which she lays her eggs. Pheasants wander over farmland, feeding mainly on grains, seeds, berries, and insects.

The chicks are well camouflaged, like their mother.

DUNNOCK
Sometimes called the hedge sparrow, the dunnock is not related to a sparrow at all – it just looks like one. Dunnocks nest in hedgerows, where they build cup-shaped nests.

The gray head and underparts help to tell the dunnock from a sparrow.

FOREST AND WOODLAND

ABOUT THE HABITAT

WITH PLENTY OF FOOD and safe nesting places, forests and woodlands provide a rich habitat for birds, from the treetops right down to the forest floor. A greater variety of birds live in the deciduous and eucalyptus woodlands than in the dark coniferous forests, because of the more favorable climates.

EURASIAN JAY

FOOD AND FEEDING

Woodland birds feed on buds, berries, and seeds from the trees and shrubs. Some eat insects and small animals. Diets may vary with changes in season.

BIRDSONG

Most woodland birds, such as the nightingale, have loud songs and calls to attract mates, and establish breeding territories in the thick undergrowth.

RING-NECKED PHEASANT WING

WINGS

Many woodland birds have short, broad, rounded wings to help them rise quickly into the air and avoid twigs and branches. Pheasants can fly quickly for short distances.

NIGHTINGALE

NESTS IN HOLES

Holes in trees are safe and warm places for birds such as redstarts to raise a family. In the nesting season, the adults frequently fly in and out with food for the growing young.

MALE
COMMON
REDSTART

CAMOUFLAGED
WOODCOCK

FOREST FACTS

• The northern forest called the taiga is the largest in the world.

• There are over 600 species of eucalyptus in Australia.

• Up to half of all woodland birds nest in tree holes.

• The woodpecker family has existed for over 50 million years.

CAMOUFLAGE

Many woodland and forest birds are well camouflaged to protect them from predators. The dull, mottled colors of this woodcock hide it against the decaying leaf litter of the woodland floor.

DECIDUOUS WOODLAND

IN THESE WARM, moist woodlands, a great variety of birds can live together by feeding at different levels, sharing the available food. In warm weather, the birds nest, raise young, and eat as much as they can. In cold weather, leaves fall off the trees and some birds migrate to warmer places.

Thick skull

Two toes facing forward and two backward

WOODPECKER SKULL

YELLOW-FRONTED WOODPECKER
This thrush-sized woodpecker of South America hammers into decaying tree trunks to find insect larvae and make nesting holes. It licks up insects with its long, sticky tongue.

Strong, stiff tail feathers for support

LONG-TAILED TITS
Long-tailed tits flit about on the edges of woodlands pecking insects and spiders off the leaves and bark. Outside the breeding season, the tits huddle in small groups at night to keep warm.

GREEN WOODHOOPOE
These birds probe tree trunks with their long, curved bills searching for food. They live in noisy family groups in African woodlands.

Long bill is used to find insect grubs or eggs and spiders.

The bill is broad at the base to catch insects.

SPOTTED FLYCATCHER
Perching on exposed branches, spotted flycatchers dart out to snap up passing insects. In cold weather, they migrate to warmer places, such as Africa, to find food.

Green woodhoopoes have high, cackling calls.

WHIP-POOR-WILL
During the day, this well-camouflaged bird sleeps on the woodland floor. At night, it flies near the ground catching insects.

CONIFEROUS FOREST

DARK CONIFEROUS FORESTS – the taiga – stretch across the top of the Northern Hemisphere from the tundra in the north to the more open deciduous woodlands in the south. The leaves stay on the trees all year round, but winters are bitterly cold and most birds leave for warmer places. In the short summer, they feed on berries, seeds, or insects.

CAPERCAILLIE
The capercaillie is able to eat pine needles to help it survive through the winter. Comblike fringes on its toes keep it from sinking into snow.

EURASIAN SISKIN
The restless and acrobatic siskin often hangs upside-down to pull the seeds out of pine and larch cones. Siskins are social birds and build nests high in conifer trees, where predators cannot easily reach the young birds.

The siskin feeds on the seeds of pine, larch, alder, and birch trees.

RED CROSSBILL

Crossbills use their scissor-like bill to lever apart the scales on the cones of pine, spruce, larch, and other conifers to reach the seeds. Parent crossbills cough up partly digested pine seeds to feed to their young.

PINE CONES

Scales
levered apart
by a crossbill

JAPANESE WAXWING

These birds are named for the red waxlike tips on some of their flight feathers. Waxwings eat berries or fruit, but will also catch insects when they can. They migrate south in the autumn in large numbers.

Waxwings
live in
large flocks

Male and
female birds
are similar
in color.

AMERICAN BALD EAGLE

Bald eagles live in forests near water where they hunt for fish and waterbirds. They do not grow the white feathers on the head and tail until they are four years old.

EUCALYPTUS WOODLAND

IN THE EVERGREEN eucalyptus woodlands of
Australia, there is food and shelter for a variety
of unique birds all year. The birds
help to pollinate the trees and
shrubs and spread their seeds.
In the rainy season, waterbirds
gather in marshy areas on the
border of these woodlands.

MALLEEFOWL
These birds build a huge mound
of rotting vegetation covered
with sand to keep their eggs
warm. The male checks the
temperature with his bill.

*Strong, hooked
beak characteristic
of parrot family*

*Two toes in
front and two
toes behind*

RAINBOW LORIKEETS
Noisy flocks of rainbow lorikeets feed
high in the trees. They crush the flowers
of eucalyptus and other flowering trees to
soak up the sticky mixture of nectar and
pollen with their fringe-tipped tongues.

Large, broad-based bill to catch and swallow prey

Large head and bill with brown ear patch

LAUGHING KOOKABURRA
Named for its very noisy, chuckling calls, the laughing kookaburra is a giant kingfisher that rarely eats fish. Instead, it pounces on reptiles such as snakes, small mammals, birds, and invertebrates.

OWLS

MOST OWLS hunt at night. Their sharp hearing and keen eyesight help them catch prey such as mice and small birds. Many owls roost in trees and have brown feathers for camouflage.

Feathers are fanned out to make owl look frightening.

SCOPS-OWL
Almost impossible to spot because of its superb camouflage, the scops-owl eats large insects. Here, it is seen defending itself from an enemy.

In a complete pellet, animal fur and bones are all stuck together.

Owl mucus binds pellet together.

OWL PELLETS
Once or twice a day, owls cough up pellets containing indigestible bits of their last meal, such as fur or bones. Pulling a pellet apart reveals what an owl has eaten.

Owl facts

• Order *Strigiformes*
• About 174 species
• Mainly nocturnal
• Birds of prey
• Eat birds, insects, and small mammals
• Habitat: mainly woodland
• Nest in tree holes or other bird's nests
• Eggs: white

SOUTHERN BOOBOOK
This small Australian owl gets its name from its double hoot. It feeds mainly on insects.

Large feet with hooked talons

BARN OWL

A heart-shaped face is the trademark of the barn owl, a bird so different from other owls that it is in a separate family. The disk of feathers on the face collects sounds like a radar dish. Barn owls make a haunting shrieking sound.

Owls catch and kill prey with their sharp talons.

"Ears" are only tufts of feathers.

EURASIAN EAGLE-OWL

The largest of all owls, eagle owls are powerful hunters, strong enough to attack hares and mallards. They have very loud hoots: male eagle owls can be heard hooting over ½ mile (1 km) away.

BARN OWL FEATHER

TAWNY OWL FEATHER

OWL FEATHERS

Soft, velvety feathers with fringes on the flight feathers muffle the sound made by the wings in flight.

Thick covering of soft feathers

RAIN FORESTS

ABOUT THE HABITAT

TROPICAL RAIN FORESTS are the richest bird habitats. They provide a wealth of food and safe nesting places, and a warm, wet climate throughout the year. Rain forest birds usually have short, broad wings to twist and turn easily when flying through the trees. This unique habitat is under threat from forestry, mining, dams, and farming.

CANOPY

UNDERSTORY

FOREST FLOOR

BIRDS OF PARADISE
Male birds of paradise have ornate and colorful feathers to attract females. They live only in the dense rain forests of northeastern Australia and Papua New Guinea.

LAYERS OF LIFE
The birds live at different levels in the trees. In this way, they share the available food and nesting places, so a huge variety of birds live close together.

SPREADING SEEDS
Fruit-eating birds such as aracaris and parrots help to spread the seeds of rain forest trees. They feed on fruits and pass the seeds in their droppings.

Wide tail helps the aracari to balance on branches

CHESTNUT-EARED ARACARI

Long bill with serrated edge

Groups of crested oropendolas hang their woven nests from tree branches.

NESTING

To keep their nests out of sight and out of reach of predators, rain forest birds nest high in the trees or in dense thickets above the ground. Some, such as parrots and hornbills, nest in tree holes.

COLOR

The bright colors of rain forest birds like these macaws are surprisingly hard to see among the leafy trees. These birds are feeding on mineral-rich soil.

HABITAT FACTS

• Since 1945, over half the rain forests have been destroyed; an area the size of a soccer field is cut down every second.

• Rain forests contain over 50 percent of all plant and animal species.

• One-fifth of all the kinds of birds in the world live in the Amazon rain forest.

UNDER THE CANOPY

BENEATH THE GREEN ROOF of the forest is the dark, cool understory of smaller trees, shrubs, and climbing plants, and below this, the leafy forest floor. There is less food and warmth at these lower levels than up in the canopy, so there are fewer birds. Large birds such as trumpeters and cassowaries stalk across the forest floor. In the understory, hummingbirds and jacamars flit through the branches.

HOATZIN CHICK

HOATZIN
Groups of hoatzins live along riverbanks in the rain forests of South America. They are poor fliers and make short, noisy flights through the trees.

Chick has claws on its wings for climbing

DOUBLE-WATTLED CASSOWARY
This huge cassowary melts into the forest if it senses danger. Males make loud, booming calls during courtship. The horny casque on its head is used to push aside forest undergrowth.

SUNBITTERN
This bird is named for the sunset colors on its wings, visible during its courtship display. At other times, it is well camouflaged by the mottled gray and brown colors of its feathers.

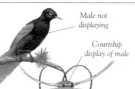

Male not displaying

Courtship display of male

BLUE BIRDS OF PARADISE
The male blue bird of paradise performs a dramatic upside-down display to show off his iridescent feathers to a female. He also makes a series of loud, vibrating notes. Females look after the young on their own.

These birds live in the middle or upper levels of the rain forest, rarely coming down to the ground.

ASIAN FAIRY-BLUEBIRDS
Noisy fairy-bluebirds move busily through the trees searching for fruit, such as figs. The metallic blue of the male is not easy to see in the shade of the trees.

Fairy-bluebirds often make sharp, whistling calls.

IN THE TREETOPS

HIGH UP IN THE RAIN FOREST CANOPY it is light and warm and there is plenty of food, especially fruits, seeds, and insect life. Bird life includes large bird predators such as eagles which patrol the treetops looking for prey. Canopy birds, such as parrots and toucans, climb well and have strong feet for grasping branches.

Bare, orange-yellow face and bill

HARPY EAGLE
The huge harpy eagle is one of the most powerful birds of prey. It swoops into the canopy to seize monkeys (like this capuchin), birds, sloths, and reptiles. It can fly very fast through the branches.

LADY ROSS'S TURACO
This African turaco lives in small, noisy groups, usually high in the canopy. Although clumsy fliers, turacos are good at running along tree branches. They make a great variety of cackling and croaking calls.

TOCO TOUCAN

This is the largest toucan, with
a bill up to 7½ in (19 cm) long. The bill
is hollow with supporting struts, so it is
not as heavy as it looks. The colors
help it to recognize other toucans
and find a mate.

ORANGE-BELLIED LEAFBIRD

This Asian leafbird helps to
pollinate the forest trees as
it feeds on nectar. It also
spreads the seeds
of plants in the
mistletoe family
by eating the
berries.

*This leafbird is
good at
mimicking other
birds' songs.*

*The casque is a thin layer
of skin and bone over
a honeycomb structure.*

GREAT HORNBILL

The hornbills of Southeast Asia and
Africa look like the toucans of South
America because they live and feed in
a similar way. They are named for the
horny casques on their bills. No-one
knows how these bony growths are used.

PARROTS

MOST PARROTS are brightly colored and live in tropical forests. They tend to fly about in flocks, making harsh, screeching calls. Many species are threatened by habitat destruction. There are three main groups: the lories, the cockatoos, and the parrots.

Narrow, tapering wings to fly fast through the trees

CANARY-WINGED PARAKEET
This small parrot's long tail helps it balance as it flies. Larger parrots usually have broad, rounded wings and fly more slowly. One parrot, the kakapo, cannot fly at all.

CHATTERING LORY
The chattering lory spends most of its time high in the trees feeding mainly on pollen and nectar. Lories have a long tongue with a brushlike tip which picks up pollen as they drink.

YELLOW-CRESTED COCKATOO
Cockatoos raise and lower their head crests when they are excited, frightened, or angry. They also do this when landing on a perch.

PARROT FACTS
• Family: *Psittacidae*
• About 330 species
• Diurnal
• Tropical land birds
• Eat fruits, seeds, nuts, and other plant parts; also some invertebrates
• Habitat: forest, scrub, grassland, and mountains
• Nest: usually tree hole, hole in bank or among rocks

ECLECTUS PARROTS

These parrots are unusual because the bright red female is such a different color from the green male. Males and females mostly look alike. Eclectus parrots feed on fruits, nuts, and leaf buds.

Nutcracker bill to crush seeds and nuts

SKULL AND BILL

Parrots have large, broad skulls with a fairly big space for the brain – they are intelligent birds. The top bill curves sharply down, fitting neatly over the broad bottom bill, which curves upward.

Many parrots have green feathers to camouflage them in the leaves of the trees.

Two toes point forward and two backward to give a powerful grip.

RIVERS, LAKES, AND SWAMPS

ABOUT THE HABITAT

WATERY HABITATS are home to a
rich variety of birds, from ducks,
coots, and rails to herons and
storks. There are plenty of
plants, invertebrates, and fish for
birds to eat, and safe nesting
places in reeds and on riverbanks.
Many birds rest and feed on
lakes, marshes, and swamps during
migration. But drainage schemes,
dams, acid rain, and pollution
from farms and factories
threaten these habitats.

COMMON
KINGFISHER

WEBBED FEET
Many waterbirds, such as Canada
geese, have webbed feet to push
the water aside as they swim.
Long legs to wade in deep
water and long toes to
walk over soft mud
are other common
features of
waterbirds.

CANADA
GOOSE
FOOT

HUNTING FOR FISH
To catch fish, birds like this kingfisher dive
into the water to seize their prey. Others,
such as herons, stand still and catch fish
that swim past. Another technique is to
scoop up fish from the surface.

CATCHING FISH
Birds need strong bills and feet to hold
slippery prey. Mergansers' bills have
serrated edges to help them
keep a strong grip on
fish they catch.

HOODED MERGANSER SKULL

NORTHERN
SHOVELER

FILTER FEEDING
Birds like the shoveler
filter tiny floating plants
and animals from water.
The shoveler has "combs"
on its bill to trap food.

CAMOUFLAGE
The dark, mottled colors of some
birds, such as the buff-banded
rail, help to
camouflage them
as they skulk
noiselessly through the reed
beds of marshes and swamps.

BUFF-
BANDED
RAIL

NESTING
Hiding a nest from predators is a relatively easy
task in these habitats. Nesting materials such as
dried reeds are also easy to find. Some birds even
build floating platforms
of vegetation for
extra security.

HABITAT FACTS

• Lake Baikal in
Siberia is the oldest
freshwater lake –
25 million years old.

• About six percent
of the Earth's surface
is covered by marshes,
bogs, and swamps.

• One-fifth of all the
freshwater on Earth
flows through the
Amazon River daily.

COOT
NESTING IN
REEDS

RIVERS AND LAKES

THESE FRESHWATER habitats are important for birds, especially in undisturbed areas free of pollution. Some birds prefer the still waters of ponds and lakes while others, such as dippers, are adapted to move in fast-flowing waters. Around the edge of the water are many places to nest and a variety of food for the young, including water insects.

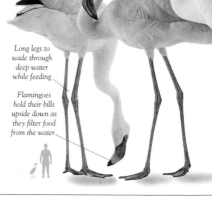

GRAY WAGTAIL
The busy gray wagtail patrols mountain streams, darting out to snap up flying insects in its long bill. It has sharp claws to grip slippery rocks and wet branches.

CLARK'S GREBES
The courtship dance, like that of the Western grebe, is elaborate. In it, a pair of grebes stands up tall and races fast across the water with heads tilted forward.

Long legs to wade through deep water while feeding

Flamingoes hold their bills upside down as they filter food from the water

At the last moment, the feet swing forward to grasp the fish.

OSPREY

The osprey is a powerful hunter, plunging feet first into water to snatch fish from near the surface. It sometimes goes right under before pulling up into the air again. Stong claws and spines under the toes help it hold slippery fish.

WHITE-CROWNED FORKTAIL

These Asian birds live by rocky streams, perching on boulders wagging their long tails. They have a loud, high-pitched whistle to communicate above the noise of the water.

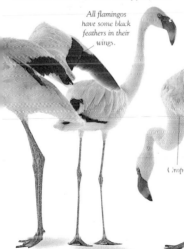

All flamingos have some black feathers in their wings.

Lesser flamingos are the smallest of the six species of flamingo.

Crop

LESSER FLAMINGOS

Flamingos live in noisy colonies, sometimes containing thousands of birds. They nest on mounds of mud, and both parents feed the young on a rich "milk" produced in the crop.

SWAMPS AND MARSHES

WET, TREELESS GRASSLANDS, called marshes, and waterlogged forests, called swamps, are often given the name "wetlands." They can be fresh- or saltwater habitats. Fish-eating birds, such as egrets and pelicans, are common, but a lot of birds can feed together by eating different kinds of food at different levels in the water. Rare birds often find refuge in wetlands since large mammal predators cannot easily hunt there.

SCARLET IBIS
Spectacular flocks of scarlet ibises feed, roost, and nest together in the tropical swamps of South America. Scarlet ibises feel in soft mud or under plants for insects, crabs, shellfish, frogs, and fish. Young scarlet ibises have gray-brown backs for a year while they mature into adults.

Long, thin, down-curved bill to probe for food

Slim body to slide easily through dense vegetation

BLACK CRAKES
These East African birds have long, widely-spaced toes to keep them from sinking into the mud and help them walk over floating water plants. Their thick bills are too short to probe in mud, so they peck small invertebrates and seeds off the surface.

BEARDED PARROTBILL

Active and acrobatic bearded parrotbills fly low over reed beds on their rounded wings. They feed on insects in warm weather, and seeds in cold weather. Both parents build the nest in the reeds and share the care of their young.

WHOOPING CRANES

Among the world's rarest birds, the whooping crane spends the winter on the coastal marshes of Texas. In spring, it migrates to Canada to breed.

Male has black mustaches

A bird's "knee" is really its ankle, so it bends backward, just like a person's ankle.

DUCKS

WEBBED FEET and broad, flat bills are distinctive
features of ducks. These birds are good swimmers and
strong fliers. There are two main types of duck –
dabbling ducks, such as the mallard,
that feed on the surface, and diving
ducks, such as the pochard. Many
ducks migrate to avoid
cold weather.

FEMALE

MALE

DOWN FEATHERS
Female ducks pluck down
feathers from their breasts
and use them to line their
nests and cover the eggs
to keep them warm.

*Short legs set well
back on body*

MANDARIN DUCKS
These ducks live near ponds
and lakes surrounded by woods, and
nest in tree holes. The male is more
colorful than the female,
except when he molts his
feathers once a year.

WOOD DUCK
Found in North America, wood ducks are related to Asian mandarin ducks. The females look after the nest, eggs, and ducklings on their own.

The ducklings swim soon after hatching.

DUCK FACTS
• Family: *Anatidae* includes ducks, swans, and geese
• About 150 species
• Diurnal
• Waterfowl
• Eat water plants and small water animals
• Habitat: ponds, lakes, rivers, or the sea
• Nest: built near water, or in tree holes
• Eggs: white or pale

DIVING DUCKS
These ducks have shorter, rounder bodies than ducks that feed on the surface. Diving ducks, such as this pochard, can stay underwater for 30 seconds or more.

PLUMED WHISTLING-DUCK
Whistling-ducks live in the tropics and look more like geese than ducks. They feed mainly on the surface.

MALE
MALLARD

Webbed feet used like paddles for swimming

MALLARD
These dabblers feed on the surface of the water or upend themselves to reach plant and animal food a little way below the surface. Mallards are the ancestors of most domestic ducks.

Wide, flat bill to sift food out of water

SEAS, CLIFFS, AND SHORES

ABOUT THE HABITAT

SOME SPECIALLY adapted birds spend most of their
lives gliding over the open oceans. But they nest on
shores and in the safety of cliff ledges, usually in large
colonies. The rich feeding
grounds of estuaries
attract huge numbers
of waders and wildfowl,
especially on migration.

FLIGHT
Seabirds such as the fulmar
have long, narrow wings
to glide fast over the
waves for long distances.
However, they are not
very good at walking,
and are clumsy
and ungainly
on land.

FULMAR IN
FLIGHT

*Fulmars have tube-
shaped nostrils above
the bill. Albatrosses
and petrels are also
tube-nosed birds.*

*Fulmars have a
stiff-winged flight,
hardly bending their
wings at all.*

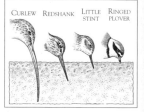

CURLEW   REDSHANK   LITTLE   RINGED
                      STINT   PLOVER

FEEDING
Finding food out at sea
is not always easy, and
seabirds spend most of
their time looking for
the next meal. Terns
dive to take fish at or
near the surface. Other
seabirds, such as puffins,
dive underwater.

PUFFIN
WITH
CATCH

SHARING FEEDING PLACES
Some shorebirds can feed close
together without competing
because their bills are different
lengths. The curlew's long bill
reaches worms in deep burrows,
while the ringed plover picks
insects off the surface.

HERRING
GULL EGGS

Most seabird eggs are more pointed at one end than the other.

CAMOUFLAGED EGGS

Birds such as gulls or terns that nest in the open on beaches or dunes have camouflaged eggs. The spots and other markings help the eggs to blend into the background so predators find it hard to see them.

NORTHERN
GANNET

HABITAT FACTS

• Oceans cover about 70 percent of the Earth's surface.

• The sea cools more slowly than the land, keeping coastal areas warmer in winter.

• The tidal range in open oceans is only about 20 in (50 cm).

• In 10 sq ft (1 sq m) of estuary there may be over 1,000 worms.

NESTING

Many seabirds nest in tightly-packed colonies of thousands or even millions of birds. The vast numbers stimulate them to breed at the same time. Gannets nest close together in noisy, smelly colonies.

ESTUARIES AND SHORES

APART FROM CLIFFS, other areas
along the shoreline, such as dunes
and beaches, provide nesting
areas for seabirds. Where rivers
meet the sea, the shallow
waters of estuaries teem with
food such as fish, worms,
and shellfish. Estuaries
are also important in
cold weather, when
inland feeding areas
are frozen.

PURPLE SANDPIPER
Stocky purple sandpipers
migrate south in colder
weather to feed on rocky
shores. They search the
shoreline for food, finding
their prey by sight rather
than by touch.

BLACK-NECKED STILT
This stilt has
extremely long legs
that allow it to feed
in deeper water than
other shorebirds.
However, it prefers to
feed in shallow water
and on muddy shores,
using its long bill to
catch insects and small
aquatic creatures.

*In flight, the
stilt's legs stick
out 7 in (18 cm)
beyond the tail.*

SLEEPING
On an estuary, shorebirds
such as this dunlin feed when
they can, and sleep when
the tide comes in and covers
their feeding grounds. They
flock to the safety of high-
tide roosts, like small islands.

INCA TERN

This South American tern often gathers in flocks of many thousands, and roosts on sandy beaches. Inca terns are graceful fliers, hovering over the sea and dipping down to snatch food from the surface.

Inca terns may follow whales and seals to seize scraps of food.

GREAT BLACK-BACKED GULL

These huge gulls are fierce predators of seabird colonies on the coast. They have long, powerful wings for gliding.

RINGED PLOVER

As soon as the ringed plover stops moving, its colors make it hard to see among the pebbles on the beach. Females may pretend to be injured to draw predators away from eggs and young.

SEA AND CLIFFS

OVER THE OPEN OCEAN, seabirds search for food, also landing on the surface to rest and preen. Seabirds have waterproofed feathers, webbed feet for swimming, and sharp bills to catch slippery prey. Many nest on cliffs where eggs and young are safe from predators.

NESTING SPACE

To share the nesting sites on a cliff, the birds nest at different levels. Alcids, such as razorbills and murres, gannets, and kittiwakes nest near the top.

After fishing, cormorants hold their wings open to dry.

NORTHERN GANNET SKULL

To catch fish, gannets plunge into the sea like torpedos from heights of up to 100 ft (30 m). They have a strong skull to withstand the impact when they hit the water with such a great force.

GREAT CORMORANT

With feathers that trap very little air and heavy bones, the great cormorant sinks in water more easily than other seabirds, and can feed on bottom-dwelling creatures.

A frigatebird robs a tropicbird of its fishy meal.

PIRACY AT SEA
Frigatebirds steal much of their food from other birds such as pelicans and gulls. They are speedy fliers and can swoop, dart, soar, and hover better than most other seabirds.

Nests of grass, seaweeds, and mud sit snugly on narrow ledges.

KITTIWAKES
These small gulls nest close together in colonies consisting of hundreds of birds. They are named after their call. Unlike other gulls they are rarely found on land

DESERTS, SCRUB, AND GRASSLANDS

ABOUT THE HABITAT

IN THESE MAINLY HOT, dry habitats, birds may have to travel long distances to find food and water, or migrate to avoid dry seasons. Seeds and insects are the main sources of food, but some larger birds also feed on reptiles, small mammals, and dead animals. In the heat of the day, most birds are less active and rest in the shade.

Bee-eaters feed mainly on honeybees.

INSECT EATERS

Birds such as bee-eaters and warblers feed on the insects that are most abundant during a rainy season. In the dry season, insect eaters often have to migrate to find enough to eat.

ROADRUNNER

White-throated bee-eaters fly to wetter grasslands in the dry season.

WHITE-THROATED BEE-EATER

VARIED DIET

Food is often hard to find, so birds survive by eating any food they come across. Reptiles are a common source of food. This roadrunner has caught a lizard.

These birds are threatened by the caged bird trade.

SEED EATERS

Grass seeds are a vital source of food for many birds, such as these Australian Gouldian finches. When the grasses die back in the dry season, the finches migrate toward wetter areas on the coast.

GOULDIAN FINCHES

GARBAGE CLEAN-UP

The carcasses of large grazing animals and human dumps provide food for birds such as marabou storks. Despite the harsh habitat, there is plenty to eat.

BURROWING OWLS

UNDERGROUND SHELTERS

To keep out of the heat of the Sun, burrowing owls rest and nest safe from enemies inside burrows dug by small mammals like prairie dogs.

MARABOU STORK

HABITAT FACTS

• More than a quarter of all the land on Earth is covered in grass.

• Deserts have less than 10 in (25 mm) rain a year.

• In Death Valley, in the Southwest, temperatures reach 131°F (55°C).

• The African ostrich is the heaviest, tallest, and fastest running bird in the world.

DESERTS

BIRDS THAT LIVE in deserts have to get most of their water either from their food or by flying long distances. By day, they may rest in the shade of rocks, or inside cacti or underground burrows. Some come out to feed at night, when it is cooler. Many birds of prey survive in deserts on a diet of reptiles and small mammals.

BLACK-BELLIED SANDGROUSE
These birds are strong fliers and travel many miles to find water. The males carry water back to their chicks in their belly feathers.

Hooked beak typical of bird of prey

ELF OWL
The sparrow-sized elf owl nests in holes dug out by woodpeckers inside giant saguaro cacti. The spines of the cactus protect the eggs and young from predators. Elf owls hunt for insects in the cool of the night.

It is much cooler inside the cactus.

HARRIS' HAWK
A fearless hunter of birds, lizards, and small mammals, Harris' hawk sometimes feeds on carcasses, alongside vultures and caracaras. It is often found near roadsides in the desert regions of the Americas.

The female does not have orange cheek patches and her bill is a duller red.

The male has zebralike stripes on the chest.

ZEBRA FINCHES
These lively little birds are common in the Australian outback. They nest after the rains when there are plenty of seeds and insects to feed to their young. They live in flocks of up to 100 birds, and several may nest together.

SCRUB AND BUSH

THE BIRDS OF these warm, dry, dusty habitats may roam widely in search of food, or follow the rains. The thorny bushes and shrubs often form dense thickets and these make safe nesting places. The berries that grow on the shrubs can be a useful source of food in colder weather for many species.

COCKATIELS

These small cockatoos wander over the Australian bush country looking for fruits and grass seeds. They usually nest after rainfall at any time of year.

Males have brighter markings on the face than the females.

BLUE-CAPPED CORDON BLEU

Small groups of cordon bleus search the ground for grass seeds and insects in the thorn scrub of East Africa. They feed their young mainly on a protein-rich diet of insects.

Short, stubby bill to crush seeds

GRAY FRANCOLIN
These birds are common in southern Asia because they are able to survive in dry conditions. They usually live in small family groups, and feed on weed seeds and grain crops. In warm weather, they also eat insects.

Francolins try to escape danger by running.

SCRUBLAND
The scrubland habitats of small trees and thorny shrubs are halfway between grassland and woodland. They include the Mediterranean scrublands, the Californian chaparral, and the bush, or outback, of Australia.

EMU
Small flocks of flightless emus roam widely through the Australian bush in search of seeds, berries, and insects. The male looks after the chicks for up to 18 months.

WHITE CRESTED HELMETSHRIKE
Tame and active white crested helmetshrikes live in small flocks of two to 20 birds. They hop through the African bush snapping up insects and spiders with their strong, hooked bills.

GRASSLANDS

A VARIETY OF seed- and insect-eating birds live in grasslands, especially those birds that can adapt to living near people. Some birds follow herds of grazing animals to snap up the insects disturbed by their feet. Other birds feed on the animals when they die. Long legs enable birds such as ostriches and rheas to see over tall grasses and watch for danger.

RED-BILLED OXPECKERS
Using their sharp claws to cling to the skin of large mammals such as giraffes and zebras, red-billed oxpeckers pick off ticks and insects living in their fur.

In breeding plumage, male is bright chestnut, with black head and throat.

This weaver is a shy bird with a fast, dashing flight.

CHESNUT WEAVER
These weavers nest in dense colonies in the African grasslands. Out of the breeding season, both male and female are dull brown.

OSTRICH
Able to survive in very dry conditions, ostriches stride over the African savannah on their long legs, searching for leaves, seeds, and insects. They are threatened by hunting and habitat destruction.

Bare head
and neck

HOODED VULTURE
The bare head
and neck of the
hooded vulture allow it to
reach right inside an animal
carcass to feed without getting
its feathers dirty. Vultures fly
high, using their sharp eyesight
to spot carrion.

It is sometimes called
the "ovenbird"
because its nest looks
like an old-fashioned
baker's oven.

Strong talons
cling onto branch

RUFOUS HORNERO
There are few trees on the South
American pampas grasslands, so the
rufous hornero builds a huge nest of mud
and straw. The nest dries, forming a hard
"birdhouse" to protect the eggs and young.

113

Mountains
and
Moorlands

ABOUT THE HABITAT

MOORLANDS TEND TO BE WET, boggy places while mountains can be very cold and windy. Only a few hardy birds live on mountains and moorland because of the harsh climate and lack of food, especially in the cold seasons. However, these habitats are important breeding areas for birds.

This shy, secretive bird rarely emerges from the bamboo thickets and dense forest where it lives.

SEASONAL MIGRATION
Hardy pheasants such as this Lady Amherst's pheasant live in the mountain forests of Asia. They move up and down the mountains with the seasons. Many pheasants are threatened by hunting.

Feathered feet to insulate against the cold

Colorful feathers and neck ruff

LADY AMHERST'S PHEASANT

CAMOUFLAGE
In autumn, ptarmigans grow new white feathers for camouflage. These tough birds bury themselves in snow to keep out cold, biting winds. In summer, their plumage is mottled gray-brown.

NESTING
CURLEW

MOUNTAIN FORESTS
The warmer forests on the lower slopes of mountains provide many birds with plenty of food and nesting places. In colder weather, birds may move down to these forests from the upper slopes.

RUFOUS-
BELLIED
NILTAVA

These Asian flycatchers live in mountain forest above 3,000 ft (1,000 m)

NESTING PLACES
Shorebirds such as this curlew nest on windswept moorlands in summer. They hide their nests among grasses and bushes. Their young feed on insects, worms, frogs, and snails. In winter, they move to the coast

GROUSE
EGG

MOORLAND EGGS
Heavy blotches of color help to camouflage the eggs of moorland nesters such as grouse and shorebirds among the heather and bracken. The eggs are laid in a shallow scrape on the ground.

CURLEW
EGG

Male has long tail for display

HABITAT FACTS
• The Appalachians were formed over 250 million years ago; the Himalayas formed only 40 million years ago.

• The world's longest mountain chain is the Andes at 4,500 miles (7,250 km) long.

• Some moorlands are created by a change to a wetter climate; others by people clearing trees for farmland.

MOUNTAINS

IN COLD WEATHER food is scarce on mountains, but these areas are undisturbed breeding areas for birds. Birds' feathers keep them warm when it is freezing cold, and efficient lungs enable them to get enough oxygen from the thin air. Many mountain birds are large and powerful fliers.

RAVEN
These powerful birds are among the largest members of the crow family. They patrol mountain slopes searching for food with their sharp eyes.

WALLCREEPER
This nimble bird clings onto rock faces with its sharp claws, probing for insects with its slender bill. In cold weather, it moves to lower slopes where there are more insects for it to eat.

SWORD-BILLED HUMMINGBIRD
This hummingbird lives high in the Andes. It has a very long bill, which it uses to sip nectar from flowers.

SNOW, ICE, AND ROCK

GRASSY MEADOWS

CONIFEROUS FOREST

TEMPERATE FOREST

HABITAT ZONES
Mountains have a variety of habitats. There are warm, deciduous forests on the lower slopes, cooler coniferous forests higher up, and, just below the snow covered peaks, grasslands and scrub.

The lammergeier is also called the bearded vulture.

LAMMERGEIER
Soaring over the mountain slopes on rising warm air currents, the lammergeier searches the steep slopes for animals killed by the harsh climate. It drops the skeleton bones on rocks to smash them open, then scoops out the marrow with its long tongue.

Lammergeiers fly to great heights and drop bones onto rocks to break them apart.

ANDEAN CONDOR
The world's heaviest bird of prey, the Andean condor has very keen eyesight. It has the longest wingspan of any land bird and soars over the Andes looking for dead, sick, or wounded animals to feed on. There is a ready supply of food because of the difficult living conditions.

MOORLANDS

THIS WATERLOGGED, tundralike habitat is found
in cool, upland areas with lots of rain. It is an
important breeding ground for shorebirds and
grouse. Predators such as harriers and golden eagles
find many small birds and mammals to eat here, and
there are plenty of
insects breeding in
the peaty bogs.

*Golden-plovers
feed on
insects, worms,
and seeds.*

*The upper parts
of this species
have golden
color all year.*

EURASIAN GOLDEN-PLOVER
In late spring, golden-
plovers migrate to
moorlands to breed. They
lay their well-camouflaged
eggs in a shallow scrape
in the ground.

STONECHAT
The restless stonechat perches on bushes and posts to watch for insects, worms, and spiders. It builds a nest of moss, grass, and hair, well hidden in bushes or thick grass.

PEREGRINE FALCON
These falcons swoop at an incredible speed to kill prey such as golden-plovers or pigeons with their talons. They pluck the feathers from prey before eating the flesh.

RED GROUSE
This bird is a distinctive subspecies of the willow ptarmigan. Many moorlands are carefully managed to keep a lot of these birds for shooting in the autumn grouse season.

Birds such as red grouse shelter, hide, and nest in heather.

Some stonechats migrate to warmer places in cold weather.

EAGLES

WITH THEIR SHARP eyes, huge wings, and strong legs and feet, eagles are the most powerful of the birds of prey. Females are larger than males. Many species of eagle are threatened by people hunting them, poisoning them, and destroying their habitat.

Light-colored crown and neck feathers

Strong talons to grip and crush prey

COURTSHIP
During courtship, many eagles show off their amazing flying skills. A pair of bald eagles will tumble and spin through the sky, while trying to touch or grip one another's talons.

Courtship display of bald eagles

IMPERIAL EAGLE
Feathered legs are a characteristic of the imperial eagle, which belongs to a group called the booted eagles. It is widespread in parts of Asia, but rare in Europe.

GOLDEN EAGLE
These eagles are strong fliers, soaring high on outstretched wings to search for prey. They are named for the golden feathers on the top of the head and the back of the neck.

Large primaries for power and steering

BATELEUR

This eagle's name comes from the French word for "juggler" because of its aerial courtship display. It has long wings and a short tail. When it is excited or angry, it raises its crest.

Raised crest

A bald eagle's eyrie

EYRIE

Eagle nests are called eyries and bald eagles have made some of the biggest eyries in the world. They use the same nest year after year, adding more and more twigs and sticks each time they nest.

EAGLE FACTS

• Family: *Accipitridae* – includes hawks and kites as well

• About 63 species

• Diurnal

• Birds of prey

• Eat a variety of animals, alive and dead

• Habitat: wide range

• Nest: mass of sticks in tree or on cliff ledge

• Eggs: white or marked with brown

POLAR
AND TUNDRA
REGIONS

ABOUT THE HABITAT

THE FROZEN POLAR REGIONS are the coldest and windiest places on Earth. Few birds can survive there all year around. Most migrate there to breed in the short summer months, when the sun shines 24 hours a day and there is plenty of food. These unique habitats are threatened by mining, tourism, and pollution.

TUNDRA LANDSCAPES

Around the edge of the Arctic Ocean lie the flat tundra lands, which have a frozen layer called permafrost under the ground. In summer, the soil above the permafrost thaws out, and lakes and marshes form on the surface.

Tundra means "barren land" in Finnish.

Ice floating on water

Shoreline

Tundra with permafrost under the ground

Marshy tundra landscape in summer

DOVEKIE

MIGRATION

In summer, millions of ducks, swans, and geese, such as the barnacle goose, migrate to the tundra lands to feed and nest there. They eat new vegetation sprouting from the warm, moist ground.

ADAPTATIONS

The Arctic alcids, such as dovekies look like the Antarctic penguins. They have flipperlike wings for swimming, but can fly.

126

KEEPING WARM

Birds such as the eider duck cover their eggs with soft down which the female plucks from her own breast. This helps to keep the eggs warm until they are ready to hatch.

PENGUIN FLIPPER

SWIMMING

Many birds of these habitats are good swimmers. Penguins have stiff, densely packed scalelike feathers on their wings to reduce the drag of the water against them when swimming.

EIDER NEST

LAPLAND LONGSPUR

FACTS

• Antarctica has 90 percent of all the ice on Earth and 70 percent of all the water.

• Permafrost under the tundra can be up to 3,840 ft (1,400 m) thick.

• The Arctic is an ice-covered ocean surrounded by land – Antarctica is frozen land surrounded by ocean.

FOOD

The tundra summer is brief, but thousands of insects swarm over marshy pools. So birds like the Lapland longspur have plenty of food to collect for their young.

ARCTIC AND TUNDRA

AROUND THE NORTH POLE is a huge ice-covered ocean surrounded by tundra landscape. This region is called the Arctic. In summer months, gulls, auks, and terns feed on the fish at sea, and nest on the coast. The insects and seeds on the tundra are food for shorebirds, ducks, geese, and small songbirds. Before winter, the birds fly south to warmer regions.

Male giving his mate a fishy gift during courtship

ARCTIC TERNS
After courtship, terns raise their young in the Arctic summer, then fly all the way to Antarctica for the summer there. They do an incredible round trip of 22,000 miles (35,400 km).

SNOWY OWL FOOT

SNOWY OWL
The plumage of the snowy owl camouflages it against the Arctic landscape, as it glides over the ground looking for prey. Feathers on its legs and feet help it to keep warm.

COMMON REDPOLL
This little bird can survive low
temperatures. It eats a lot of seeds,
and some small insects and their
larvae in summer. Some redpolls
nest in dwarf birches near the
ground in tundra habitats.

*Redpolls are named
after their red
forehead, or "poll."*

EMPEROR GOOSE
This handsome gray goose breeds
along marshy shores in Alaska.
Some birds may migrate
south to northern
California in
winter.

*Adults have
orange legs.*

*In winter, the male
snow bunting turns
browner and looks more
like the female.*

SNOW BUNTING
Hardy snow buntings breed in
the Arctic – farther north than
any other perching bird.
They usually hide their
nest from predators
in crannies in
the rocks.

*Snow buntings
may burrow in
the snow to
escape intense
cold.*

ANTARCTICA

THIS VAST AREA of frozen land surrounded by ocean has little rain or snow, so the birds have little fresh water to drink, apart from melted snow. The only two landbirds are sheathbills. All the others are seabirds, including albatrosses, petrels, and penguins, millions of which nest around Antarctic coasts in summer. The seabirds have dense feathers or layers of fat to keep warm, and are strong swimmers or fliers.

ANTARCTIC SKUA
With their hooked bills and strong claws, skuas are fierce predators of penguin eggs and chicks. In summer, they regularly invade penguin colonies in Antarctica.

ADELIE PENGUINS
Adelies are one of the two species of penguins that nest on the rocky coasts of Antarctica itself. In spring, they march inland from the sea to nest on the ground in huge rookeries.

BLACK-BROWED ALBATROSSES
Albatrosses mate for life and reinforce the pair bond each year when they return to the nest. This pair is bill-touching and preening each other.

The only bird found in Antarctica that does not have webbed feet

SNOWY SHEATHBILL

A relative of shorebirds, this bird scavenges around seal and penguin colonies as well as searching the shoreline for fish, invertebrates, and shellfish. Sheathbills live in small flocks, except in the breeding season.

IMPERIAL SHAGS

These cormorants nest in large colonies on coastal ledges or among rocks. They have strong, hooked bills to grasp slippery fish. In the breeding season, they grow wispy crests.

BLACK-BROWED
ALBATROSSES

Nest is a big heap of mud and grass about 24 in (60 cm) high

PENGUINS

WITH THEIR SMOOTH, streamlined shape, and stiff, strong wings, penguins are expert swimmers. They dive to catch fish and squid with their spiky tongues. Dense, oily feathers and thick fat under the skin keep them warm in the cold southern oceans.

Penguins only come out of the water to molt and breed, some in colonies of 500,000.

EMPEROR PENGUINS
These are the biggest penguins. They never come on land, but breed on the ice that floats around Antarctica in winter. Males incubate the single egg for about nine weeks.

KING PENGUINS
The striking golden orange ear patches of these birds are used for display during courtship. The markings also help them to recognize other king penguins. These large birds can dive down as deep as 850 ft (250 m).

Powerful, narrow wings for swimming

Stiff tail feathers used to support body on land

Male king penguin incubates egg against bare patch of warm skin.

*Porpoising
Adelie penguins*

*In the water,
penguins look dark
from above and
pale from below
– this helps to
camouflage them.*

SWIMMING AND DIVING

In order to breathe while swimming fast, penguins leap in and out of the water. This technique is called porpoising. They can travel through water in this way at over 20 mph (30 km/h), using their stiff wings to push themselves along.

MACARONI PENGUIN

During their courtship displays, these birds shake their bright yellow head crests. The crests also help them to recognize other macaronis.

*Spread
flippers
cool bird
down*

PENGUIN FACTS

- Family: *Spheniscidae*
- About 17 species
- Diurnal and nocturnal
- Flightless seabirds
- Eat fish, squid, and small sea creatures
- Habitat: southern oceans, cool temperate islands, tropical shores
- Nest: stones, grass, mud, caves, or burrows
- Eggs: whitish

*Feet well
back on
body to act
as rudder*

CHINSTRAP PENGUIN

These penguins are named because of the black line under their chin. They are noisy and quarrelsome birds

REFERENCE
SECTION

BIRD CLASSIFICATION

THE PROCESS OF CLASSIFICATION puts living things, such as birds, into groups based on features that they have in common. It is a way of organizing our knowledge about birds, and may or may not consider their evolutionary history. Birds are divided into a series of increasingly narrow categories, starting at the level of class.

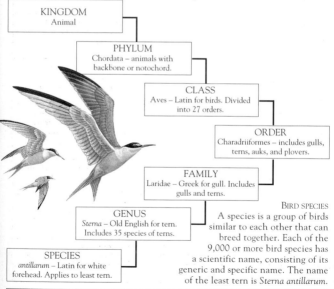

KINGDOM
Animal

PHYLUM
Chordata – animals with backbone or notochord.

CLASS
Aves – Latin for birds. Divided into 27 orders.

ORDER
Charadriiformes – includes gulls, terns, auks, and plovers.

FAMILY
Laridae – Greek for gull. Includes gulls and terns.

GENUS
Sterna – Old English for tern. Includes 35 species of terns.

SPECIES
antillarum – Latin for white forehead. Applies to least tern.

BIRD SPECIES
A species is a group of birds similar to each other that can breed together. Each of the 9,000 or more bird species has a scientific name, consisting of its generic and specific name. The name of the least tern is *Sterna antillarum*.

ORDER	COMMON NAME	CHARACTERISTICS
STRUTHIONIFORMES *(approximately 1 species in order)*	Ostrich	Large flightless African bird, long neck and legs, two toes
RHEIFORMES *(approximately 2 species in order)*	Rheas	Large, flightless South American birds, three toes
CASUARIIFORMES *(approximately 4 species in order)*	Cassowaries and emu	Large, flightless Australasian birds, three toes
APTERYGIFORMES *(approximately 3 species in order)*	Kiwis	Medium-sized, flightless New Zealand birds, nocturnal, good sense of smell
TINAMIFORMES *(approximately 46 species in order)*	Tinamous	Gamebird-like species from Central and South America, poor fliers, ground-dwelling
SPHENISCIFORMES *(approximately 18 species in order)*	Penguins	Flightless, swimming seabirds with flipperlike wings, webbed feet, dense plumage, usually blue-black above, white below
GAVIIFORMES *(approximately 5 species in order)*	Loons	Large swimming and diving birds, with webbed feet, pointed bill, and long, thin neck
PODICIPEDIFORMES *(approximately 21 species in order)*	Grebes	Small- to medium-sized swimming and diving birds, with lobed feet, pointed bill, and long, thin neck
PROCELLARIIFORMES *(approximately 110 species in order)*	Albatrosses, fulmars, petrels, shearwaters, storm-petrels, diving-petrels	Seabirds with tubelike nostrils, good sense of smell, long wings. Come to land only to breed, slow development

ORDER	COMMON NAME	CHARACTERISTICS
PELECANIFORMES *(approximately 62 species in order)*	Tropicbirds, pelicans, gannets and boobies, cormorants and shags, darters and anhingas, frigatebirds	Fish-eating, mostly marine birds with three webs linking four toes. Some have expandable throat pouch
CICONIIFORMES *(approximately 117 species in order)*	Herons and bitterns, storks, ibises and spoonbills, hamerkop, whale-headed stork, flamingoes	Large wading birds with long legs and long bill, eat mainly fish and amphibians, also large insects. Flamingoes are filter feeders
ANSERIFORMES *(approximately 150 species in order)*	Screamers, ducks, geese, swans	Semiaquatic wildfowl with well-developed down, a feathered oil gland, and round, open nostrils
FALCONIFORMES *(approximately 290 species in order)*	Vultures, osprey, hawks and eagles, secretary bird, falcons and caracaras	Small to large diurnal birds of prey; some scavengers (vultures), others hunters (falcons)
GALLIFORMES *(approximately 274 species in order)*	Megapodes, curassows and guans, pheasants and grouse, turkeys, guineafowl	Ground-dwelling gamebirds. Young leave nest soon after hatching
GRUIFORMES *(approximately 190 species aim order)*	Mesites, button quails, plains-wanderer, cranes, limpkin, rails, coots, trumpeters, finfoots, kagu, sunbittern, seriemas, bustards	Ground-dwelling, many live in wet habitats, most nest on ground or make floating nests
CHARADRIIFORMES *(approximately 337 species in order)*	Shorebirds, gulls, terns, skuas, skimmers, auks	Diverse group of aquatic, often marine birds, often web-footed, variety of bills
COLUMBIFORMES *(approximately 300 species in order)*	Pigeons, doves, sandgrouse	Landbirds with long, pointed wings, short legs, small feet, small head and bill
PSITTACIFORMES *(approximately 342 species in order)*	Parrots, lories, cockatoos	Colorful tropical landbirds with powerful hooked bill, four toes (two front and two back). Often long-lived, some good mimics

ORDER	COMMON NAME	CHARACTERISTICS
CUCULIFORMES *(approximately 159 species in order)*	Turacos, cuckoos, anis, roadrunners, hoatzin	Landbirds with four toes (two front and two back), bill not hooked. Some cuckoos parasitic. Hoatzin unique
STRIGIFORMES *(approximately 174 species in order)*	Barn owls, owls	Mostly nocturnal or crepuscular birds of prey with good hearing, large, immovable eyes, facial disk, silent flight, strong talons
CAPRIMULGIFORMES *(approximately 109 species in order)*	Oilbird, frogmouths, potoos, owlet-nightjars, nightjars	Mainly nocturnal or crepuscular birds with camouflaged colors and wide bill to scoop up insects. Oilbird feeds on fruit
APODIFORMES *(approximately 429 species in order)*	Swifts, tree swifts, hummingbirds	Agile fliers with very short upper arm and small feet. Hummingbirds tiny nectar-feeders with fast wingbeats
COLIIFORMES *(approximately 6 species in order)*	Mousebirds	Small, African birds with long, pointed, graduated tails, short wings and legs, and stout, hooked bill
TROGONIFORMES *(approximately 39 species in order)*	Trogons	Mainly fruit-eating, tropical forest birds, with small, weak feet and legs, long, squarish tail, brightly colored plumage
CORACIIFORMES *(approximately 204 species in order)*	Kingfishers, rollers, motmots, bee-eaters, rollers, ground rollers, cuckoo roller, hoopoe, wood-hoopoe, hornbills	Carnivorous landbirds with large bills. Usually brightly colored with two front toes joined for all or part of their length
PICIFORMES *(approximately 381 species in order)*	Jacamars, puffbirds, barbets, honeyguides, woodpeckers	Four toes (two forward and two back), many forest dwellers, variety of bill shapes and sizes
PASSERIFORMES *(approximately 5,414 species in order)*	Includes pittas, starlings, swallows, leafbirds, birds of paradise, thrushes, warblers, chickadees, sunbirds, finches	Largest order with 75 families and 60 percent of all birds. Perching landbirds with four toes (three forward, one back)

BIRDWATCHING

TO REALLY UNDERSTAND birds, you need to watch them yourself. Choose warm, waterproof clothes that are well camouflaged, and take a notebook. A pair of binoculars is vital; a camera or tape recorder may also be useful.

YOU WILL NEED

NOTEBOOK

TAPE RECORDER

BINOCULARS
8 X 30 MM

CAMERA
35 MM SLR

BLINDS
Birds are (with good reason) suspicious of people. To get close to them, you will need to hide behind bushes or fences, and stalk quietly and slowly. The best cover is a blind, especially when the birds are nesting. A car can make a good blind.

*Vertical slit in wall
for watching birds*

*Old sheet or canvas
painted green or brown*

*Framework of sticks
tied with string or wire*

FLIGHT SHAPES

You may only catch a glimpse of many birds, especially birds of prey, flying high overhead. Learning to recognize flight shapes like the ones below will help you to identify birds even when you cannot see them clearly.

Eagle – wide wings and tail, fingerlike wingtips

Heron – bowed wings, head tucked back, feet trailing

Swallow – long, forked tail, pointed wings

Gull – long, narrow wings

KEEPING A NOTEBOOK

Sketching the birds you don't know will help you identify them later, and you don't have to be able to draw well. First draw a rough outline of the bird; then note its color, shape, flight pattern, and behavior. You can also jot down where and when you saw the bird, and what the weather was like.

Goose – wide wings with pointed tips, neck stretched out

Crow – broad, pointed wings with slotted tips, long tail

BIRDWATCHING CODE

• Always avoid disturbing birds, particularly if they have eggs or young.

• Never touch, handle, or collect eggs and nests.

• If you see a baby bird on its own, leave it alone; one of its parents is probably nearby.

TRACKS AND SIGNS

YOU WILL NEED

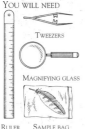

TWEEZERS

MAGNIFYING GLASS

RULER   SAMPLE BAG

STUDYING TRACKS and signs that birds leave behind will tell you a lot about their behavior and diet. Food remains, feathers, eggshells, and droppings provide clues, as do footprints. Pellets, the undigested remains of a bird's meals, are also useful signs. Birds of prey produce pellets, but so do other birds such as gulls, shorebirds, and crows.

FEATHERS
You may find feathers that have been molted, or discarded after a bird has been eaten.

SHOREBIRD   CROW   SONGBIRD

PELLETS
Good places to look for bird pellets include nest sites, feeding sites, and roosting places.

RECORDING TRACKS
A plaster cast of a bird track gives an accurate record which you can build up into a permanent collection. Plaster of Paris is available at most hardware stores.

JUG OF WATER   BOWL AND SPOON   PLASTER OF PARIS

STRIP OF INDEX CARD   PAPER CLIPS

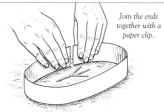

Join the ends together with a paper clip.

1 Look for a good, clear bird track left in wet mud or damp ground. Bend a strip of card around it and join the ends with a paper clip. Push the card a little way into the ground.

All of the remains belong to voles.

This is a tawny owl pellet.

CANADA GOOSE FOOTPRINTS

LEG BONES

SKULL

SHOULDER BLADE

The hard parts of creatures are not digested

TEETH

JAW

VERTEBRAE

FUR

FOOTPRINTS

Look out for webbed footprints of ducks and geese and long, widely spaced toes of herons.

PECKED APPLE

NUTS

SNAIL SHELLS

DISSECTING PELLETS

Soak the pellets in water for about half an hour and gently pull them apart with tweezers. Look for bones and the hard parts of insects.

FOOD REMAINS

Bill marks in berries or fruit, and ragged holes in shells and nuts, are clues to bird meals.

Plaster of Paris mixture

It is a good idea to note down where and when you found the track.

Brush off any dust before varnishing

2 Mix the plaster of Paris and the water in the bowl, stirring with a spoon or stick. Be careful not to make the mixture too thick. Pour it inside the card ring, over the track.

3 When the cast has set hard (about 15 minutes), lift it carefully off the ground and wrap it up to take home. Later on you can paint and varnish the cast to protect it.

FEEDING THE BIRDS

IN COLD WEATHER, you can help birds survive by putting out food. In warm weather, there is plenty of natural food about so there is less need to lend a hand. Remember to put out water as well as food.

Gaps for rainwater to drain off

Try to identify the birds that visit the table regularly

BIRD TABLE
Encourage birds to visit you by making a bird table. Hang the table from a branch or windowsill, or fix it to the end of a stake in the ground. Position the table about 4-5 ft (1.2-1.5 m) off the ground and no more than 12-16 ft (3.5-5 m) away from cover. Clean the table every so often.

YOU WILL NEED

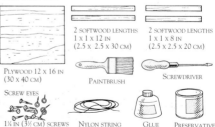

PLYWOOD 12 x 16 IN (30 x 40 CM)

2 SOFTWOOD LENGTHS 1 x 1 x 12 IN (2.5 x 2.5 x 30 CM)

2 SOFTWOOD LENGTHS 1 x 1 x 8 IN (2.5 x 2.5 x 20 CM)

PAINTBRUSH

SCREWDRIVER

SCREW EYES

1¼ IN (3½ CM) SCREWS

NYLON STRING

GLUE

PRESERVATIVE

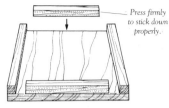

Press firmly to stick down properly.

1 Glue the four thin strips of wood or dowel to the edges of the plywood, as shown. There should be a gap in each corner.

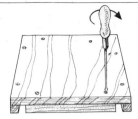

2 Turn the table over and screw the sides down to hold them firmly in position. Put in two screws on every side as shown.

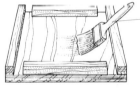

Press hard on the paint brush

3 Paint the wood with a wood preservative that is not harmful to wildlife. Allow it to dry completely before the next step.

4 Put two screw-eyes at the base of each short side and thread string or nylon thread through the holes. Your bird table is ready to hang.

BIRD FOOD

A wide range of food will attract a variety of birds. For a bird pudding, mix food such as seeds or nuts with the same amount of melted suet or fat.

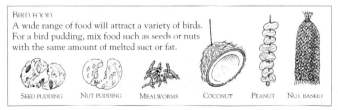

SEED PUDDING   NUT PUDDING   MEALWORMS   COCONUT   PEANUT   NUT BASKET

ENDANGERED BIRDS

OVER TEN PERCENT of the world's birds are endangered and about half of these live on islands. The parrot family is the most at risk, with over 70 species threatened. In the past, people have hunted some birds, such as the passenger pigeon and the dodo, to extinction. Today, hunting is still a threat to birds, but other human activities, especially habitat destruction, are a far greater danger to their survival.

HABITAT DESTRUCTION
About two-thirds of the world's birds are threatened by people draining wetlands, cutting down forests, and plowing grasslands. More areas need to be set aside as bird sanctuaries.

POLLUTION
Oil slicks at sea, acid rain falling on forests or lakes, the use of pesticides on farmland – all this pollution threatens birds. The planet would be a healthier place if pollution was reduced.

HUNTING AND COLLECTING
Hunting birds for food or feathers, or collecting their eggs, has reduced their numbers considerably. We could help birds by banning the hunting of rare species and migrating birds.

INTRODUCED SPECIES
People have often introduced animals such as cats, rats, and mongooses into places they visited or settled. These introduced species compete with native birds and hunt them.

BIRD TRADE
Many people keep colorful birds in cages as pets. Some are taken from the wild, and many die in transit. Of every ten birds caught, only about one reaches the pet shop.

ISLAND BIRDS
Many rare birds are found only on certain islands, such as the Galapagos, Hawaiian islands or Madagascar. They are especially threatened because their numbers are so low.

NAME	REGION	REASON FOR EXTINCTION
HYACINTH MACAW	Brazil, Paraguay, and Bolivia	
DALMATION PELICAN	S.E. Europe and southern Asia	
KAKAPO	New Zealand	
WHOOPING CRANE	North America	
ESKIMO CURLEW	North and South America	
IVORY-BILLED WOODPECKER	Cuba	
GURNEY'S PITTA	Southern Burma and peninsular Thailand	
NOISY SCRUB-BIRD	Western Australia	
WHITE-TAILED EAGLE	Eurasia	
JAPANESE CRESTED IBIS	Japan and eastern China	
MAURITIUS KESTREL	Mauritius	
KAGU	New Caledonia	
BLACK PARADISE FLYCATCHER	Seychelles	
GREAT PHILIPPINE EAGLE	Philippines	
JUNIN OREBE	Chile and Argentina, south to Tierra del Fuego	

BIRD RECORDS

BIRDS HAVE DEVELOPED some remarkable adaptations of size, movement, appearance, and nesting behavior. The following examples are some of the more amazing record-breakers.

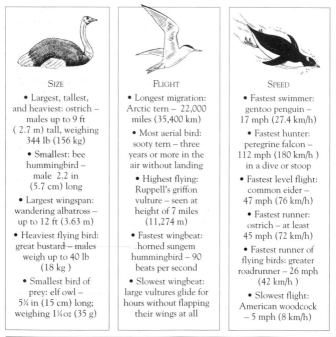

SIZE

- Largest, tallest, and heaviest: ostrich – males up to 9 ft (2.7 m) tall, weighing 344 lb (156 kg)
- Smallest: bee hummingbird – male 2.2 in (5.7 cm) long
- Largest wingspan: wandering albatross – up to 12 ft (3.63 m)
- Heaviest flying bird: great bustard – males weigh up to 40 lb (18 kg)
- Smallest bird of prey: elf owl – 5¾ in (15 cm) long; weighing 1¼ oz (35 g)

FLIGHT

- Longest migration: Arctic tern – 22,000 miles (35,400 km)
- Most aerial bird: sooty tern – three years or more in the air without landing
- Highest flying: Ruppell's griffon vulture – seen at height of 7 miles (11,274 m)
- Fastest wingbeat: horned sungem hummingbird – 90 beats per second
- Slowest wingbeat: large vultures glide for hours without flapping their wings at all

SPEED

- Fastest swimmer: gentoo penguin – 17 mph (27.4 km/h)
- Fastest hunter: peregrine falcon – 112 mph (180 km/h) in a dive or stoop
- Fastest level flight: common eider – 47 mph (76 km/h)
- Fastest runner: ostrich – at least 45 mph (72 km/h)
- Fastest runner of flying birds: greater roadrunner – 26 mph (42 km/h)
- Slowest flight: American woodcock – 5 mph (8 km/h)

FEATHERS

- Fewest: hummingbirds – less than 1,000
- Most: swans – more than 25,000
- Longest: quetzal's tail feather is more than twice the length of its body

NESTS

- Most intricate: African weaverbirds
- Largest tree nest: bald eagle – width 9 ½ ft (2.9 m); depth 20 ft (6 m)
- Smallest nest: bee hummingbird – thimble-sized
- Largest communal nest: sociable weaver – up to 300 nest chambers

EGGS

- Smallest: bee hummingbird – ¼ in (6.35 mm) long
- Biggest: ostrich – up to 7 in (17.8 cm) long
- Largest clutch: gray partridge – 15–19 eggs
- Incubation: wandering albatross – 75–82 days

BILLS

- Longest: Australian pelican – 1 ½ ft (47 cm)
- Longest bill compared to body length: sword-billed hummingbird – 4 in (10.2 cm)
- Broadest: shoebill or whale-headed stork – width 5 in (12 cm)
- Sideways curving: wrybill of New Zealand

LIFESPAN

- About 75% of wild birds live less than a year
- Longest-lived banded seabird: royal albatross – 60 plus
- Oldest captive bird: sulphur-crested cockatoo – 80 plus

SONG

- Most talkative: an African gray parrot "Prudle" – 800 words
- Best mimic: marsh warbler can copy songs of 60 or more other birds
- Loudest: male three-wattled bellbird and the kakapo – calls carry for 0.6 miles (1 km)

Resources

There are more than 1,000 bird clubs in the US and Canada, many of which are local chapters of larger organizations such as the National Audubon Society. To inquire about the club nearest you, contact one of the following, or the local natural history museum.

US ORGANIZATIONS

National Audubon Society
700 Broadway
New York, NY 10003

American Birding Association (ABA)
P.O. Box 6599
Colorado Springs, CO 80934

Many local bird clubs maintain rare bird alert hotlines that describe birds seen in the area. A complete list of these telephone numbers is available from the ABA.

American Ornithologists' Union (AOU)
National Museum of Natural History
Smithsonian Institute
Washington, DC 20560

Cornell Laboratory of Ornithology
159 Sapsucker Woods Rd.
Ithaca, NY 14850

The Nature Conservancy
1815 North Lynn St.
Arlington, VA 22209

National Wildlife Federation
1400 16th St., NW
Washington, DC 20036

World Wildlife Fund
1250 24th St. NW
Washington, DC 20037

CANADA ORGANIZATIONS

Canadian Nature Federation
Suite 606
1 Nicolas St.
Ottawa, K1N 7D7

Canadian Wildlife Federation
2740 Michael Cowpland Drive
Kanata
Ottawa, K2M 2W1

Canadian Wildlife Service
Place Vincent Massey
351 St. Joseph Blvd.
Hull, QUE K1A 0H3

SOME PLACES TO WATCH BIRDS

Obtain further information by writing the refuge.

US LOCATIONS

(NWR: National Wildlife Refuge)

Aransas NWR
P.O. Box 100
Austwell, TX 77950

Assateague Island National Seashore
7206 National Seashore Lane
Berlin, MD 21811

Bosque del Apache NWR
P.O. Box 1246
Socorro, NM 87801

Bombay Hook NWR
2591 Whitehall Neck Rd
Smyrna, DE 19977

Cape Hatteras National Seashore
1401 National Park Drive
Manteo, NC 27954

Cape May Bird Observatory
707 East Lake Drive

Cape May Point, NJ
08212

Chautauqua NWR
19031 E. County Road
Havana, IL 21 ON

Des Lacs Refuge Complex
8315 Hwy 8 Kenmare,
ND 58746

Everglades National Park
40001 State Road 9336
Homestead, FL 33034

Flint Hills
P.O. Box 128
Hartford, KS 66854

Gateway National Recreation Area
Public Affairs Office
210 New York Avenue
Staten Island
NY 10305

Hart Mountain National Antelope Refuge
P.O. Box 21
Plush, OR 97637

Klamath Basin Refuges
4006 Hill Road
Tulelake, CA 96134

Ninigret Refuge Complex
Shoreline Plaza, Route 1A
P.O. Box 307
Charlestown, RI 02813

Nisqually NWR Complex
100 Brown Farm Road
Olympia, WA 98516

Okefenokee NWR
Rt. 2, Box 3330
Folkston, GA 31537

Parker River NWR
261 Northern Blvd.
Plum Island
Newburyport, MA 01950

Point Reyes Bird Observatory
4990 Shoreline Hwy
Stinson Beach, CA
94970

Santa Ana NWR
Route 2, Box 202 A
Alamo, TX 78516

Savannah Coastal Refuges
Parkway Business Center
Drive
Suite 10
Savannah,
GA 31405

CANADA
LOCATIONS

Beaverhill Bird Observatory
P.O. Box 1418
Edmonton, ALB
T5J 2N3

Cold Lake Provincial Park
P.O. Box 8208
Cold Lake, ALB
T9M 1N1

Cap Tourmente National Wildlife Area
Saint-Joachim, QUE
G0A 3X0

Churchill Northern Studies
P.O. Box 610
Churchill, MB, R0B 0E0

Creston Valley Wildlife Management Area
P.O. Box 640
Creston, BC V0B 1G0

Delta Marsh
Delta Waterfowl
Research Station
R.R. 1
Portage la Prairie,
R1N 3A1

Point Pelee National Park
R.R. 1
Leamington, ONT
N8H 3V4

Riding Mountain National Park
Wasagaming, MB
R0J 2H0

Glossary

ACID RAIN
Rain that has more acid than normal because of the chemicals from cars, power stations, and factories dissolved in it.

ADAPTATION
Evolutionary process by which living things become fitted to their environment.

AIRFOIL
A wing that is curved on top and flat underneath.

ALTRICIAL
Helpless, blind young birds, with few feathers, which stay in a nest and rely on their parents for food and warmth.

BARB
Branch from the central shaft of a feather.

BARBULE
Branch from the barb of a feather with tiny hooks along it.

BIRD OF PREY
Common name given to birds that hunt and kill other animals for food. They have hooked bills, talons, and keen senses.

BINOCULAR VISION
Seeing and focusing with both eyes at once.

BROOD PATCH
Featherless area of thickened skin on the underside of a bird's body, used to keep eggs warm during incubation.

CAMOUFLAGE
Colors, markings, or patterns which help living things blend in with their surroundings.

CASQUE
Bony extension of the top part of the bill.

CLUTCH
Set of eggs laid by one female and incubated together.

COLONY
Large number of birds which gather together to breed or roost.

COURTSHIP
Ritual display that takes place before mating.

COVERTS
Groups of small feathers that cover the base of major flight feathers.

CREPUSCULAR
Active at dusk.

CROP
Saclike extension of a bird's gut used to store food; often used to carry food back to the nest.

DIGESTION
The process by which food is broken down so it can be absorbed into the cells that make up living things.

DIURNAL
Active during daylight.

DOWN
Very soft, fine feathers which help trap air and keep a bird warm.

EGG TOOTH
Structure on the tip of the upper bill with which a chick cracks open the eggshell to hatch.

EXTINCTION
The process by which living things die out of existence.

FLIGHT FEATHERS
Large feathers which make up the wings and can be divided into primary (on the outer wing) and secondary (on the inner wing).

FOLLICLE
Cavity in a bird's skin out of which a feather grows.

GIZZARD
Muscular chamber in the stomach where food is ground up.

INCUBATION
Act of sitting on eggs to keep them warm.

INVERTEBRATE
Animal without a backbone.

IRIDESCENCE
Changing color with position; colors often shiny like a rainbow.

KERATIN
Protein from which feathers are formed.

LIFT
The force of air that keeps things airborne.

MIGRATION
The movement of animals from one area to another at certain times of the year to find food and warmer climates.

MONOCULAR VISION
Seeing separate images with each eye.

MOLTING
The process of shedding old feathers and growing new replacement ones.

NECTAR
Sugary liquid produced by flowers and some leaves to attract some birds for pollination.

NOCTURNAL
Active at night.

PELLET
A hard lump of indigestible pieces of food which some birds, such as owls, cough up.

PIGMENT
A substance that gives color to eggs and feathers.

PLUMAGE
A bird's feathers.

POLLINATION
The transfer of pollen from the male to the female parts of flowers or cones so that seeds can develop.

PRECOCIAL
Down-covered young birds which have their eyes open, and leave the nest soon after hatching.

PREDATOR
An animal that kills other animals for food.

PREENING
Method by which birds care for their feathers using the bill and oil from the preen gland.

RESPIRATION
The process by which living things release energy from their food.

ROOSTING
Sleeping, including resting behavior when birds are not actually asleep.

SPECIES
A group of similar birds that can breed together to produce fertile young.

SYRINX
Sound-producing organ in birds, situated where the windpipe joins the tubes leading to the lungs.

TALONS
Sharp, curved claws of birds of prey.

TENDON
Band or cord of tough tissue connecting a muscle with a movable structure such as a bone.

TERRITORY
Area which a particular bird occupies and defends against other birds of the same species.

THERMAL
Rising column of warm air, used by soaring birds for extra lift.

Species index

Index

Acknowledgments

Dorling Kindersley would like to thank:
Hilary Bird for the index, and Joseph DiCostanzo, Helen Hays, Richard Thomas, and Steven Wendt for technical advice.

Photographs by:
Dennis Avon, Simon Battensby, Jane Burton, Peter Chadwick, Philip Dowell, Mike Dunning, Neil Fletcher, Frank Greenaway, Steve Gorton, Dave King, Colin Keates, Cyril Laubscher, Nick Parfit, Karl Shone, Kim Taylor, Harry Taylor, Jerry Young

Illustrations by:
Angelika Elsebach, Mark Iley, Richard Orr, Maurice Pledger, Colin Salmon, Kevin Toy, John Woodcock

Picture credits: t = top b = bottom c = center l = left r = right
Dennis Avon 38b, 81bl;110bl.
Bruce Coleman 28c;106bl;Jen and Des Bartlett 31 tl;/Patrick Clement 134-135;/Dr. M.T. Kahl 108tr;/Cyril Laubscher 42br;/Jan van de Kam 100br;/ Luiz Claudio Mango 61tr; George Mcarthy 89b;117tl;/Rinie van Meurs 100 tr;/Bruce Nielson 143 tr;/Charlie Off 90bl;/Hans Reinhard 118cl;129b; 133bc;

Kim Taylor 59b;69cl.
Corbis: Tony Arruza 56cr
F.L.P.A./E&D Hosking33t;/130-131; 133 cr/ T&P Gardner;/
F.Polking 58br;/Silvestris 88tr;/Roger Tidma 119t;/ Roger Wimshurst 61tr;/ W,Wisniewski 127 br.
Robert Harding 96-97;119b.
NHPA /Melvin Grey 23cl; /Peter Johnson 130 bl;/John Shaw 112r; 114-115.
Nature Photographers 41tr;/H. Miles 126bl;/Paul Sterry 103 r;/Derek Washington 64-65.
Oxford Scientific Films/Doug Allen 132 l.
Papilio 48br;/Larus Argentatus 26-27; 76-77.
Planet Earth Pictures 10-11; /Sean Avery 104-105;/Andre Barttschi 79 bc;/John Lythgou 62b;111tr;/Mark Mattock 98-99;/Hector Rivarola 113bl; Yuri Shibbnev 67tl.
Kim Taylor 24-25 b.

Every effort has been made to trace the copyright holders and we apologize in advance for any unintentional omissions. We would be pleased to insert the appropriate acknowledgement in any subsequent edition of this publication.